David Bennett is a senior barrister and head of chambers at Liverpool Civil Law, 1 Old Hall Street, Liverpool.

During his long career at the Bar he has practised in many different areas of law, including housing conditions litigation, but for the last 10 years he has concentrated solely on housing conditions work in which he has a very busy practice.

His decision to write this practical guide was motivated by two factors.

First, he considers this to be a very important area of law in which the lay clients are heavily reliant on the expertise of all the professionals concerned, namely solicitors, barristers and surveyors. In many cases the lives of tenants and their families are often badly affected by their housing conditions, causing discomfort, inconvenience, frustration, and not infrequently ill-health. He regards the work therefore as very important, and for many tenants, life changing.

Secondly, he has acquired a great deal of knowledge and expertise in housing conditions work over many years and feels that he needs to pass on this expertise to the relevant professionals some of whom may be new to this area of law, so that the work done at all levels by the experts involved, is of the highest quality to ensure the best result for the lay client.

Housing Conditions Claims on Behalf of Social Housing Tenants

A Practical Guide for Solicitors, Barristers and Surveyors

Housing Conditions Claims on Behalf of Social Housing Tenants

A Practical Guide for Solicitors, Barristers and Surveyors

David Bennett
Barrister, Middle Temple,
BA (Hons).

Law Brief Publishing

Published 2023 by Law Brief Publishing, an imprint of Law Brief Publishing Ltd
30 The Parks
Minehead
Somerset
TA24 8BT

www.lawbriefpublishing.com

Paperback: 978-1-914608-92-6

PREFACE

This practical guide is aimed at assisting the professionals involved in housing conditions litigation on behalf of social housing tenants. Essentially, that means solicitors and the various fee earners working in solicitors' offices, barristers, and surveyors.

To those not familiar with landlord and tenant law, this may be a new or relatively new area of practice for them. It must be emphasised however that this work is not a law textbook in the conventional sense, but is a guide to the litigation process. There are of course a number of well-known textbooks dealing with landlord and tenant law, but the one that most if not all practitioners will be familiar with, and which is devoted solely to the niche area of disrepair/housing conditions is the excellent and invaluable work entitled "Housing Conditions tenants' rights" by HHJ Jan Luba KC, Catherine O'Donnell, and Giles Peaker, now in its 6th edition, hereinafter referred to for ease as "Luba et al". Reference is periodically made to that book, and all lawyers practising in this area of law are encouraged to purchase a copy, if they do not already have one. It is with respect and thanks to the learned authors of that work that reference is occasionally made.

Experience has shown that not only do the various lawyers involved in housing conditions litigation need some useful pointers as to how the litigation on behalf of tenants is most effectively to be conducted, but so do the surveyors whose practice encompasses this type of work, and which is an essential corollary to it. However, because many of them too are new to preparing reports for litigation purposes, and specifically for this type of litigation, they also welcome guidance which will make their professional task easier and correctly focused. Accordingly, part of this work is aimed specifically at surveyors.

The law is stated to be correct and up to date as at 1 March 2023.

Finally, again for the sake of ease, the Landlord and Tenant Act 1985 is generally referred to as "the 1985 Act". The Pre-Action Protocol for

Housing Conditions Cases (England) is generally referred to as "the Protocol". All references to solicitors and fee earners, barristers, and surveyors are expressed in the masculine gender, purely for conciseness of style. Absolutely no offence is intended, and hopefully none is taken, and it is of course fully acknowledged that all the professionals at whom this guide is aimed will be both males and females.

This area of the law has gone through some interesting and long needed recent changes, in particular the addition of new provisions in the 1985 Act dealing with unfitness for human habitation. At the time of writing the Social Housing (Regulation) Bill is still going through Parliament, and of course the tragic and avoidable death of the 2-year old child, Awaab Ishak, in Rochdale has brought all of this sharply into focus and is informing changes to the Bill.

It is to Awaab Ishak's memory that I dedicate this book.

David Bennett
Liverpool Civil Law
March 2023

CONTENTS

PART ONE

THE WORK OF THE SOLICITOR

CHAPTER ONE

THE CORRECT PARTIES

<u>Who is the tenant?</u>

This may seem an obvious question, but it is surprising how easy it is to make a mistake. Given that the action is contractual in nature, identification of the contracting party or parties is essential. The best indication will come from the tenancy agreement, but often the solicitor will not have this, as the prospective Defendant landlord has not disclosed it, and the tenant has not retained, or cannot locate, a copy.

A further problem arises due to the fact that there may be joint tenants, and the Civil Procedure Rules (CPR) require that where two or more persons are jointly entitled to a remedy, all persons jointly entitled to the remedy must be parties in the action – see CPR 19.3 (1). However, one of the tenants may have permanently ceased occupation for some reason, for example joint tenants may be divorced and only one remains. The Rules provide for this type of situation – see CPR 19.3 (2). However, the general rule is that both tenants must be Claimants in the action, and the fee earner with conduct should ensure that there is a retainer with both.

Having identified who the tenant is, consideration will need to be given as to whether there are any logistical problems. If the client speaks little or no English then ultimately the services of an official interpreter may be required. Initially a family member can help the solicitor with taking instructions – and then later help counsel in conference. An assessment will have to be made with some clients whether a litigation friend will be needed due to issues with capacity (which may require input from the client's GP or some other professional), or generally because the client would have difficulty giving or receiving instructions without assistance. Children of the tenant will of course require a litigation friend (normally the tenant) if they are to be joined as Claimants in any action where they are seeking damages for personal injury.

Who is the landlord?

This can often be problematic. The best way of ascertaining the identity of the landlord is to see how the landlord describes itself in the tenancy agreement. However, as mentioned above, tenancy agreements are not always available, either from the landlord or the tenant. Sometimes, even if they are available, they have the name of the original landlord before a sale or stock transfer to the present landlord.

Some landlords conduct all of their day-to-day affairs, including the litigation process, through an arms length management organisation (ALMO). It is easy to think that this organisation is the landlord. Experience has shown that some landlords can be less than open over their exact identity. The seriousness of this is that proceedings can mistakenly be issued against the wrong landlord. This in turn leads to the problem of having to amend pleadings (if that is even permitted by the rules in these circumstances) or of having to discontinue proceedings altogether and start again. Either scenario can be expensive and can be a waste of both time and costs. Accordingly it is essential to ascertain the correct identity of the landlord before issuing proceedings. If there is any doubt, enquiry must be made with the potential Defendant or, if represented, with its solicitors to ensure that this mistake is not made.

It is also important to check if the landlord is a limited company. Again, incorrectly naming the landlord as an unincorporated organisation will only lead to difficulties, and may well lead to discontinuance.

It should be remembered that there is a statutory remedy to assist in what may be or may become a difficult situation, albeit that this may only be a rare occurrence. Section 1 of the 1985 Act creates a summary offence and reads as follows:

"1 Disclosure of landlord's identity.

(1) If the tenant of premises occupied as a dwelling makes a written request for the landlord's name and address to—

(a) any person who demands, or the last person who received, rent payable under the tenancy, or

(b) any other person for the time being acting as agent for the landlord, in relation to the tenancy,

that person shall supply the tenant with a written statement of the landlord's name and address within the period of 21 days beginning with the day on which he receives the request.

(2) A person who, without reasonable excuse, fails to comply with subsection (1) commits a summary offence and is liable on conviction to a fine not exceeding level 4 on the standard scale.

(3) In this section and section 2—

(a) "tenant" includes a statutory tenant; and

(b) "landlord" means the immediate landlord."

CHAPTER TWO

TAKING INSTRUCTIONS

In the context of housing conditions litigation the important information which needs to be collated from the client will centre around identifying who the tenant is as discussed above, and then taking careful instructions about those issues which are central to the case. The most important details which will be needed from the client will relate to notice, i.e. what notice has been given to the landlord of disrepair/unfit housing conditions. In particular, as much detail as possible should be obtained as to the following: what disrepair or housing conditions were reported; when notice was first given and how often thereafter; how it was given – i.e. by telephone on the Defendant's disrepair helpline, by email, in person to the client's housing officer, or on the Defendant's online portal, or by visits to the local housing office.

It is not unusual for a tenant to seek help from their local councillor or their MP. If so, the client should be asked to provide, if possible, any relevant correspondence into which they have been copied, as this is good evidence of notice. Clients should also be asked if they can obtain and/or provide copies of telephone or mobile phone bills showing the number of the landlord's disrepair helpline and how frequently it has been called. This will not be possible if the Claimant has a "pay as you go" mobile phone. In essence, any evidence which the client may volunteer may be helpful in establishing notice of disrepair given to the landlord. This is often a principal area of challenge by the landlord, and therefore evidence of notice of disrepair is often key. However, courts are not slow to accept the point that tenants are generally unwilling to sit in sub-standard housing conditions, when they simply have to do no more than make a phone call to report disrepair.

Social housing tenants cannot be expected to maintain accurate records in relation to reporting of disrepair, albeit that occasionally the fee earner might encounter one that does. This is usually a bonus but is not the norm. By contrast however landlords are expected to maintain accurate records, and all claim to do so, but experience has shown that this is a far cry from reality. Indeed, the Housing Ombudsman has recently issued a press release (dated 8 November 2022) dealing with this topic. 67% of investigations which were upheld by the Ombudsman in 2021–22 involved poor record keeping by landlords.

CHAPTER THREE

THE CORRESPONDENCE PHASE

Attempt to keep correspondence to a minimum. Whilst a certain amount of correspondence is inevitable, it is a mistake to be drawn into litigating the case in this way. It is very much in the landlord's interest to attempt to do so, as firstly, it can be an attempt to put off the tenant from litigating at all, and secondly it buys time for the landlord to carry out works of repair, thus ensuring that by the allocation stage of proceedings there is no longer a claim for specific performance. This means that in many cases the claim is at risk of being allocated to the small claims track as the value of damages will be £10,000 or less (under the current Rules). An allocation to small claims inevitably has the potential for considerable costs savings for the landlord.

A tenant should not be discouraged by seemingly aggressive correspondence from the landlord. The tenant either has a good case or has not. Litigation should be conducted with appropriate alacrity due to the fact that in many cases the tenant is living in poor conditions. More will be discussed in depth in a later chapter, but a common response by landlords is that the tenant should first use the landlord's internal complaints procedure and/or use the Housing Ombudsman Service before litigating. This tactic is sometimes successful and solicitors can be discouraged from pursuing the litigation process on the basis that there is force in the landlord's approach. As will be seen in a later chapter, tenants and those representing them should not be put off by this.

CHAPTER FOUR

PRE-ACTION DISCLOSURE / SUBJECT ACCESS REQUEST

Paragraph 5.3 of the Protocol states that the Letter of Claim should also request disclosure from the landlord of all documents relevant to the disrepair. It then goes on to list five categories of disclosure. It is not uncommon for landlords to overlook or even ignore this request even though there is a duty of disclosure both under the Protocol and under the Civil Procedure Rules. At one time, pre-action disclosure applications by tenants were common in this situation. However this changed with a Court of Appeal decision in the case of *Robert Hockett v Bristol City Council.* This was the decision of Bean LJ on 20 August 2021 (reference B2/2021/1025). In essence, an appeal by the tenant against a refusal of the lower court to allow an application for pre-action disclosure was dismissed. The court said that the appropriate route in this situation was to make a Subject Access Request under the data protection legislation. If this failed or turned out to be evasive, or attempted to conceal the contents of relevant documents then the case for a renewed application for pre-action disclosure might well be strengthened. Care must therefore be taken not to pursue a pointless application for pre-action disclosure in the first instance, with inevitable costs consequences.

CHAPTER FIVE

USE OF THE LANDLORD'S INTERNAL COMPLAINTS PROCEDURE

Is it obligatory or even necessary to use the landlord's internal complaints procedure before commencing litigation?

Paragraph 4.1 of the Housing Conditions Protocol states that:

> *"The parties should consider whether some form of alternative dispute resolution procedure would be more suitable than litigation and if so, try to agree which form to use. Both the landlord and the tenant may be required by the court to provide evidence that alternative means of resolving the dispute were considered. The courts take the view that litigation should be a last resort, and that claims should not be issued while a settlement is still actively being explored...."*

Several important points arise here.

The Protocol states that the only requirement is to <u>consider</u> whether some form of ADR would be more suitable than litigation. In other words, ADR is not mandatory, but should be considered. Having considered the option, a tenant is then free to choose whether he wishes to engage in some form of ADR, or to pursue a private law remedy through litigation in the courts. Indeed, the two are not mutually exclusive, and the Ombudsman has made it clear in his report of 26 October 2021 that commencing the pre-action Protocol did not constitute legal proceedings and that ADR can be pursued at any stage of the Protocol, and that a matter does not become "legal" until proceedings have been issued. Even then, it is suggested that ADR can be attempted at any stage and indeed is encouraged by the court during the litigation process. It is not uncommon at the case management conference stage for proceedings to be adjourned for ADR to be attempted. In furtherance of the Protocol, the courts can require the landlord and the tenant to provide evidence (e.g. a witness statement) that alternative means of resolving their dispute were considered.

Tenants can and often do offer ADR in the letter of claim itself, and it would be advisable to do so. This shows a willingness on the part of the tenant to litigate as a last resort. It is further suggested that if early ADR is successful, the tenant would be entitled to his reasonable costs pursuant to the principles laid down in the case of *Birmingham City Council v Lee [2008] EWCA CIV 891*, namely that if the case is settled on terms which justify bringing it then the tenant would be entitled to his reasonable costs up until the point in time when the necessary repair work is completed. It should be remembered however that the tenant's entitlement to costs arises only if there is agreement between the parties prior to the issue of proceedings which includes costs; or ultimately, if proceedings are brought, they end in success for the tenant. This is dealt with more fully below in a separate chapter.

Tenants are often (but by no means always) put off using the landlord's internal complaints procedure as they have been let down by the landlord's attitude to its repairing obligations, which is why many tenants ultimately feel that their best option is to pursue a legal remedy. Tenants and/or their representatives should check on the Housing Ombudsman Service website (www.housing-ombudsman.org.uk) how many findings there have been against a particular landlord of service failures, maladministration or even severe maladministration. This will often be a deciding factor on whether or not to make use of the landlord's internal complaints procedure as opposed to commencing litigation.

A number of important connected questions arise.

Is the landlord's internal complaints procedure likely to result in the *necessary/appropriate* repair work being carried out, and being carried out quickly? Further, will it result in appropriate compensation being paid to the tenant? Will it deal with any alleged personal injury associated with the housing conditions? Will any repair work carried out by the landlord be "sticking plaster" in nature and not go to the root of the problem – especially with matters of dampness and mould growth. Will the internal complaints procedure be anything more than a peremptory or cosmetic exercise?

A tenant would be entitled to ask his landlord to send full written details of the internal complaints procedure, the timescales involved, and what senior members of the landlord's organisation comprise the committee which examines complaints. Also, a tenant would be entitled to request details of what, if any, recent changes had been made to the internal complaints procedure following the Social Housing White Paper published on 17 November 2020 and updated on 22 January 2021 as the "Charter for Social Housing Residents". Furthermore, a tenant would be entitled to ask the landlord to provide details of how the internal complaints procedure has been updated to comply with the Housing Ombudsman's Complaint Handling Code published in July 2020 and taking effect from 1 April 2022.

It is suggested that in the event that all of these conditions have been met, the tenant may indeed wish to pursue his complaint through the internal complaints procedure. If these conditions have not been met, he may with little difficulty come to the conclusion that pursuing a legal remedy is likely to be the preferred option.

Further, as stated in the Protocol, is a settlement still actively being explored?

This will obviously be a question of fact in every case. If settlement is actively being explored then arguably the issue of proceedings would be premature. A reasonable decision would have to be taken in every case whether correspondence and/or discussions between the parties amounts to exploration of settlement, or conversely can reasonably be described as something different. If the latter, then the issue of proceedings cannot be criticised if the tenant has chosen to pursue that course, having considered alternatives.

CHAPTER SIX

THE LANDLORD'S OBLIGATIONS UNDER THE PROTOCOL

Paragraphs 6.2 and 6.3 of the Protocol require action from the landlord in response to the letter of claim. Paragraph 6.2 is straightforward. A failure to comply with the 6.2 requirements should be dealt with as suggested above under the heading of "pre-action disclosure/Subject Access Request". Of more importance is fulfilment of the obligations under paragraph 6.3. A response is required from the landlord to the matters listed at 6.3 (a) – (f) either in the response to the letter of claim (which is rare) or alternatively within 20 working days of receipt of the report of the single joint expert, or receipt of the experts' agreed schedule following a joint inspection.

The landlord must state: (a) whether liability is admitted, and if so in respect of which defects; (b) if liability is disputed in respect of some or all of the defects, the reasons for this; (c) any point which the landlord wishes to make regarding lack of notice of the disrepair or any difficulty in gaining access; (d) a full schedule of intended works, including anticipated start and completion dates and a timescale for the works; (e) any offer of compensation; and (f) any offer in respect of costs.

Paragraph 6.4 of the Protocol states that a failure to respond within 20 working days of receipt of the letter of claim or at all, is a breach of the Protocol and the tenant is then free to issue proceedings. This is important because firstly, landlords frequently fail to deal with the matters set out in paragraph 6.3, and secondly, because they often seek to argue that the tenant has issued proceedings prematurely. Paragraph 6.4 is an important provision because it gives approval to the issue of proceedings if there has been a failure by the landlord to comply with paragraph 6.3, which is often the case. The more difficult question to answer is whether paragraph 6.3 requires a landlord to answer all 5 sub-paragraphs, or whether it only requires some to be answered. It is suggested that the landlord is required to deal with all of the sub-paragraphs, rather than being selective. Selective answering only leads to confusion, which is plainly undesirable. There is a strong argument therefore that all the sub-paragraphs must be dealt with, and once dealt with, the "roadmap" of the case will be much clearer.

CHAPTER SEVEN

THE REQUIREMENT FOR THE TENANT TO PROVIDE ACCESS TO THE LANDLORD

There are two principal sources for the proposition that a tenant must allow access to his landlord for the purposes of viewing the condition of the premises and to carry out any necessary repair work.

First, there is almost invariably a clause in the tenancy agreement imposing this obligation on the tenant.

Secondly, section 11 (6) of the Landlord and Tenant Act 1985 imposes an obligation on the tenant to allow access to the landlord upon the landlord having given at least 24 hours prior written notice. There are in fact a number of other statutory sources, most notable of which is section 16 of the Housing Act 1988 applicable to assured tenancies, which will apply to the vast majority of local authority and housing association tenancies.

At common law the landlord must be reasonable in the exercise of his licence to enter and give the tenant sufficient notice of his intention to enter, and give information as to the nature and extent of the work he proposes to carry out – see *Grenada Theatres Ltd v Freehold Investments (Leytonstone) Ltd Ch 592 at page 608.*

Accordingly, if the tenant so chooses, he is free to refuse access to the landlord unless the above conditions are complied with.

Does the tenant need to be decanted before works of repair commence?

Some works of repair are so extensive, or would be so inconvenient to the tenant and his family if carried out whilst in occupation, that it would be unreasonable not to decant the tenant to suitable alternative accommodation (perhaps a hotel) during the period of the works. Some cases will be obvious, but some less so. If the works would involve disconnection of electricity and/or the gas supply, or for example the decommissioning of a kitchen and/or bathroom during repair works, the dwelling house will obviously be uninhabitable. Whilst some tenants may choose to remain in occupation and live in an unaffected (or relatively unaffected) area of their home, most would find this difficult if not impossible and would require a decant.

Surveyors are normally instructed to consider this point in their survey report and their opinion will usually carry considerable weight. Sometimes however there may be special reasons why a tenant would need to be decanted, and this would usually be informed by health conditions or other medical needs. For example, a tenant or one or more of his children who are asthmatic could not be expected to remain in occupation in a house where a lot of plaster work is to be hacked off and then renewed. The amount of dust created by such activities is likely to be injurious to the occupants if they have respiratory conditions. A letter from the tenant's GP may be useful or indeed necessary in addition to any view expressed by the surveyor on this point.

If the parties are at loggerheads over the question of decanting, the tenant could always resort to an application under CPR Part 25 for an interim remedy, and let the court decide after considering all of the available evidence.

Landlords are often reluctant to agree to a decant unless they really have to, as this often involves them in expense (and sometimes considerable expense) especially if a family has to be decanted to a local hotel due to the unavailability of suitable alternative accommodation in the landlord's stock. Some hotels will allow the family dog also, failing which the landlord would have to pay for kennelling fees. Any transfer of white goods, TVs, phone lines, Wi-Fi etc. would all have to be paid for by the landlord. That said, both landlord and tenant would have to be reasonable in all the circumstances. It will normally be for the tenant's solicitor to conduct the negotiations in relation to the nature and timing of a decant.

If the landlord unreasonably refuses a decant, or for some reason a decant is not either possible or feasible, the tenant may be entitled to damages for breach of the implied/express covenant for quiet enjoyment.

CHAPTER EIGHT

PERSONAL INJURY

Solicitors should consider whether any of the occupants of the dwelling house have suffered personal injury as a result of the disrepair and/or housing conditions. It is surprisingly frequent how often those living in a dwelling house which is in disrepair or which is unfit for human habitation suffer some form of illness.

One of the most common illnesses encountered in these cases is a respiratory condition caused or exacerbated by damp and mould. Even to a layman this may come as little surprise, but there is an abundance of medical literature dealing with respiratory illness caused by damp and/or mould in dwelling houses. Asthma or exacerbated asthma is commonly caused by such living conditions. Whilst death from respiratory illness may be rare, it was certainly instrumental in the death of the 2-year old child Awaab Ishak in Rochdale.

Indeed, under the generic heading of "Asthma", the Judicial College Guidelines state that for a number of respiratory conditions like mild asthma, bronchitis, colds and general chest problems which usually result from poor housing conditions or similar exposure, and particularly when it concerns young children who are treated by a GP and who recover within a few months, damages are surprisingly generous at up to £5150.

Another common illness caused by poor housing conditions is depression and anxiety. Even if the cause of a tenant's depression and anxiety is multifactorial, it is common for their fragile mental health to be exacerbated by the ongoing state of disrepair of their home and the difficulties that they have encountered with their landlord in attempting to get repair work carried out. They often feel that they have been treated shabbily, or simply fobbed off for a long period of time. It is not difficult even for a layman to understand that a person with fragile mental health could suffer a worsening of their condition because of an ongoing state of disrepair of their home and their landlord's attitude to the tenant and/or its repairing obligations.

Whilst this is by no means confined to female tenants, mental ill health is a common feature in a significant percentage of cases. Female tenants are often single women living with one or more children, struggling to cope with their lives. Such tenants are vulnerable, and causation or exacerbation of mental health problems is common, and accordingly the solicitor having conduct of the case should be alive to this type of injury. Investigation can be started when initial instructions are taken from the client, or the matter can be discussed more fully in conference with counsel. Indeed it may be counsel who discusses the matter for the first time with the tenant in conference. If on balance personal injury claim is indicated either for the tenant or for one or more children as discussed above, then the tenant should be asked if they would be happy to pursue a personal injury claim in the same proceedings, and if so, to provide an authority to the solicitor to obtain their GP records and/or those of any child who may also have suffered a personal injury.

Experience has shown that most tenants are happy to pursue a claim for damages for personal injuries and a high proportion of these claims will succeed. In the case of a tenant or child with asthma, a report from an independent GP, it is suggested, will suffice, as GPs are very experienced in dealing with asthma and other common respiratory conditions. In the case of anxiety and depression, it is suggested that it would be preferable to instruct a psychologist rather than a GP.

If a decision is taken to pursue a claim for personal injuries, then in most cases (with the exception perhaps of a very minor injury) the Pre-Action Protocol for Personal Injury Claims will need to be commenced and run concurrently with the Housing Conditions Protocol. If any Part 36 offer has already been made by the solicitor to the landlord, then this should be withdrawn in writing pending the investigation of the personal injury claim.

CHAPTER NINE

THE PROTOCOL REQUIREMENTS FOR PERSONAL INJURY CLAIMS

Paragraph 3.5 of the Protocol reads as follows:

> *"Housing disrepair claims may contain a personal injury element. If the personal injury claim requires expert evidence other than a general practitioner's letter, the Personal Injury Protocol should be followed for that element of the disrepair claim. If the personal injury claim is of a minor nature and will only be evidenced by a General Practitioner's letter, it is not necessary to follow the Personal Injury Protocol. If the disrepair claim is urgent, it would be reasonable to pursue separate disrepair and personal injury claims, which could then be case managed together or consolidated at a later date."*

Usually a landlord will transfer conduct of any personal injury element in the case to its insurers. The experience of most insurers comes from dealing with road traffic accident or accident at work claims for which there is a Ministry of Justice portal through which the majority of claims will be handled, unless and until such time as a claim drops out of the portal, for various reasons.

Claims for damages for personal injury in housing conditions claims however are not dealt with through an MOJ portal, but instead are dealt with in accordance with paragraph 3.5 of the Housing Conditions Protocol as just described. Any attempt therefore by a landlord and/or its insurer to reject any claim for damages for personal injuries because it is not being conducted through the MOJ portal, should itself be rejected.

Should the main claim be delayed while the personal injury element is being investigated?

The investigation and gathering of the necessary evidence for the personal injury element can take weeks, or even months. It is suggested that the delay of the main claim is unjustified as the tenant is likely to be living in poor housing conditions, and accordingly there is an imperative for reasonable speed, especially if occupants are being made ill by these conditions. Accordingly it is suggested that the preferable way of proceeding in this situation is to conduct the housing conditions litigation in accordance with the Housing Conditions Protocol and the Civil Procedure Rules, whilst at the same time investigating the personal injury element, in particular determining whether causation can be established i.e. are the housing conditions causing the alleged personal injury? Causation is of course one of the matters which any medic preparing a report must be instructed to consider.

If proceedings are issued, then reference can be made by counsel in the pleading that a personal injury claim for one or more of the occupants of the dwelling house is being investigated and that the pleadings will be amended in due course to plead the further cause of action if causation is established.

An alternative way of dealing with this situation is for separate proceedings to be issued for personal injury after the main housing conditions proceedings have earlier been issued, and then case managed together as paragraph 3.5 of the Protocol suggests.

Accordingly the tenant's claim can be brought in the amended particulars of claim or in separate particulars of claim which are then consolidated. A personal injury claim for any other occupant, such as a child of the tenant, can be the subject of separate proceedings altogether, even after the main action has concluded successfully. It is suggested however that it would probably be more convenient overall to pursue a claim for the occupants and the tenant in the same proceedings, either by later amendment or consolidation.

If a landlord has been notified in the original particulars of claim that there may be a later amendment to the pleading to include the further cause of action for damages for personal injury, it is suggested that it would be unreasonable of the landlord to refuse its consent to the amendment. The landlord can be warned that if consent to the amendment is refused, then the necessary application to the court under CPR Part 17 and/or or Part 19 will be made, and the cost of such application sought from the landlord.

Finally, there are two other ancillary benefits to pursuing a valid claim for damages for personal injury on behalf of the tenant. Firstly, qualified one-way costs shifting (QOCS) is likely to apply to the claim – see *Brown v Commissioner of Police for the Metropolis [2019] EWCA Civ 1724.* Secondly, the addition of a personal injury claim in the housing conditions proceedings creates another layer of problems for the landlord, which understandably will be unwelcome. This may cause a landlord to make a serious and early evaluation of its position, and may perhaps focus its mind on making an early and reasonable offer in compromise of any potential proceedings.

Interim injunctions

This is a relatively rarely used remedy, but one which practitioners should know about. It is mentioned at this point because the remedy is only of relevance when there is a serious risk to health. This would extend to risk of serious bodily injury or death. It is dealt with at length by Luba et al. at paragraph 3.120 – 3.141, to which the reader is referred for an important and in-depth discussion on the topic.

It is worth stating however that in any case in which it is considered that such a remedy is appropriate, a practical way of dealing with it in the first instance is for a warning letter to be written to the landlord setting out clearly the seriousness of the situation and that an application for an interim injunction will be made unless proposals are immediately forthcoming to remedy the situation so as to remove the threat of harm etc. to the tenant and/or the other occupants of the dwelling house. It is to be hoped that such a letter would have the desired effect, but in any event it will protect the tenant in relation to any possible adverse costs order if he proceeds to seek injunctive relief when a less radical course may well have had the same effect, without satellite litigation.

CHAPTER TEN

LIMITATION

<u>What is the limitation period applicable to a housing conditions claim?</u>

The claim is contractual as it is based on a breach of an implied or an express contractual term in a tenancy agreement relating to the landlord's duty to keep a dwelling house in repair. Pursuant to section 5 of the Limitation Act 1980, the applicable limitation period is 6 years. However, when does that period start? The answer is that it starts on the date that proceedings are issued and goes back in time 6 years from that date. Any claim for damages for discomfort and inconvenience preceding that 6-year period will be statute barred by effluxion of time.

It must be remembered however that limitation is a defence and unless and until raised by the landlord, limitation does not come into operation. Accordingly, if judgement in default is obtained against a landlord either for failing to enter an acknowledgement of service or a defence, then the tenant would be entitled to claim damages going back more than 6 years if that is when the notice period commenced.

Damages can be claimed by the tenant, as just stated, for the period commencing 6 years preceding the date of issue, and going forward until such time as all of the repair work is completed, as the claim for damages is a continuing cause of action, renewing on a daily basis – see *Grenada Theatres Ltd v Freehold Investments (Leytonstone) Ltd [1959] Ch 592 at page 608.*

What is the position regarding limitation with a personal injury claim in housing conditions proceedings?

This is dealt with by Luba et al. at paragraph 3.46 to which readers are referred. The case of *Millington v Islington LBC August 1999 Legal Action 25*, and *Housing Law Casebook at paragraph R1.7 in the 7th addition* cited by Luba is of particular interest. The potential problem centres around the provisions of section 11 of the Limitation Act 1980 which applies a three-year limitation period not only to the personal injury claim, but to all causes of action in the same proceedings. There is the potential therefore for a claim for damages for discomfort and inconvenience in the housing conditions aspect of the claim to be limited to 3 years, when it could be as much as 6 years as just discussed.

There are three approaches to the problem. First, seek the landlord's agreement not to rely on the three-year limitation period. Secondly, to issue separate proceedings for the housing conditions claim and the personal injury claim and then consolidate the two. Thirdly, as in *Millington* to apply in the face of the court to extend the three-year limitation period pursuant to the court's discretion under section 33 of the Limitation Act 1980. This application was successful in *Millington*.

CHAPTER ELEVEN

HUMAN RIGHTS

As the reader knows, this is not intended to be a textbook on the law, but a practical guide to those involved in housing conditions litigation. Luba et al. deal with the subject in fairly short compass in paragraphs 2.131 to 2.139. This is certainly a good starting point on the subject.

<u>Is a cause of action alleging breach of the tenant's human rights even necessary given all the other causes of action available?</u>

It is suggested that the death of the child, Awaab Ishak, in Rochdale has brought this topic into sharp focus and made it a cause of action worth pursuing.

It should be emphasised however that the purpose of pursuing the cause of action is not to obtain further damages in a housing conditions case, but its purpose is to seek and obtain a declaration that the tenant's human rights and/or the human rights of one or more of the other occupants of the dwelling house have been breached. The last thing that a social landlord would want, and would want publicised in the media, is that that landlord has breached the tenant's human rights, including those of other occupants. It is suggested that this cause of action should probably be reserved for the most egregious type of landlord behaviour. Interestingly, in his letter of 22 November 2022, Richard Blakeway, the Housing Ombudsman said this:

> *"There has been an exponential rise in casework involving damp and mould reaching our service, with 134% more cases for formal investigation and 42% of our severe maladministration decisions involving damp and mould".*

Furthermore, in his report of 2 February 2023, the Ombudsman said that in his best estimate 0.2% of dwelling houses let by social landlords have the most serious damp and mould problems. 1% to 2% have serious damp and mould problems; and 3 to 4% have notable damp and mould problems. Given that there are over 4.4 million dwelling houses in the social housing sector, this is clearly a serious and substantial problem.

<u>What is the human right in question which is allegedly breached?</u>

Under Article 8 of Part 1 of Schedule 1 of the Human Rights Act 1998 every person has a right to respect, inter alia, for their family life and home.

Accordingly, if the conditions in a person's home are such that they could reasonably be said to be unfit for human habitation, then it is suggested that a cause of action should be included in the housing conditions proceedings alleging breach of Article 8, seeking a declaration to that effect.

Would a social landlord want to defend such litigation? Possibly yes, but probably not. Many landlords, faced with the prospect of such a finding, may be more inclined to enter into early settlement negotiations (possibly without admission of liability) rather than going to trial.

<u>Is an alleged breach of human rights a continuing cause of action or would the one-year limitation period for alleged breaches of human rights be problematic?</u>

It is suggested that it is a continuing cause of action, but even if that was ultimately held to be wrong, the court has a broad discretion to extend the limitation period, which it may well be disposed to do in a serious case.

A second situation in which it would be appropriate to consider pleading breach of human rights is when the landlord is in breach of a court order for specific performance or a Tomlin Order or compromise agreement in relation to the carrying out of repair work. This is dealt with below under the heading of Breach Proceedings.

CHAPTER TWELVE

JUDGEMENT IN DEFAULT

Solicitors make a common error when they seek judgement in default of acknowledgement of service or in default of a defence.

Simply returning the slip at the bottom of the Notice of Issue form sent out by the court (N 205B) is incorrect and the court will not enter judgement. If the court does mistakenly enter judgement, the judgement will be invalid and any application to set it aside would be bound to succeed. CPR 12.4 (3) states that the Claimant must make an application in accordance with Part 23 if he wishes to obtain a default judgement on a claim which consists of or includes a claim for any other remedy.

In the vast majority of housing conditions claims the tenant will be seeking an order for specific performance of the landlord's repairing obligations in addition to seeking damages. Accordingly, the rule just cited comes into operation.

It should be remembered that the application for judgement will be seeking not only damages, but an order for specific performance in accordance with the tenant's expert's report and Scott Schedule. If the court order granting the application comes back with the case being listed only for a determination in relation to damages at any disposal hearing, then application should be made under CPR 23.10 to have the court order varied to include the question of specific performance being determined at the disposal hearing.

CHAPTER THIRTEEN

BREACH PROCEEDINGS

What course is open to a tenant when the landlord fails to comply with a court order for specific performance, or fails to fulfil the terms of a compromise agreement, Tomlin Order or an accepted Part 36 offer?

This is dealt with by Luba et al. at paragraphs 3.200 to 3.208 to which the reader is referred.

Failure to perform works directed by a court in an order for specific performance is punishable by committal for contempt. The procedure is set out in CPR 81, and it is essential that all the requirements of that rule are carefully followed. Failure to follow the Rule 81 procedure will inevitably result in any application being rejected.

Such applications are undoubtedly serious because they are seeking a fine and/or imprisonment against the appropriate person for contempt of court in failing to obey a court order. That is why the procedure must be followed precisely. It is suggested that it would be appropriate in the first instance to fire a warning shot across the bow of the landlord by stating that if the order for specific performance is not fully complied with by a certain extended date (perhaps 21 days would be entirely appropriate) then an application under Part 81 for committal will be issued. It is to be hoped that this would have the intended effect. If it does not, the person against whom the application is made could have little cause for complaint.

Against whom would the application for committal be made?

In the warning letter just discussed, the landlord should be asked for the exact identity of the Director of Housing Services. If the Defendant fails to respond to that request, or refuses it, then it is suggested that the order should simply be issued against the Defendant's Director of Housing Services with a clause in the order that in the event that the Defendant takes issue with the person described in the Penal Notice (i.e. the Director of Housing Services) then he may apply to the court for a variation of the Penal Notice within 7 days and supply the correct identity of the responsible person.

Breach of a Tomlin Order

Tomlin Orders provide within their terms a clause for the return of a case to court without the need for issuing fresh proceedings in the event of a breach of the Order. Accordingly, the appropriate way of dealing with a breach would be to issue an N244 application for the breach to be dealt with. The application should not only seek an order for specific performance (or if appropriate damages in lieu of specific performance) but also further damages and costs.

Breach of a Part 36 settlement

CPR part 36.14 (8) states that:

> *"Where – (a) a Part 36 offer (or part of a Part 36 offer) which is not an offer to which paragraph (6) applies is accepted; and (b) a party alleges that the other party has not honoured the terms of the offer, that party may apply to enforce the terms of the offer without the need for a new claim".*

This is the appropriate way of dealing with a Part 36 offer which has not been honoured by the offeror, and it should be brought before the court, as the rule states by an application to enforce. This would be an N244 application.

Breach of a settlement (compromise) agreement

A settlement agreement, which is a common means of settling housing conditions cases, is a contract. If that contract is broken, a letter of claim should be sent to the defaulting landlord, pointing out the breach and proposing settlement terms in relation to that breach. This might be, for example, an offer to allow a further 21 days for repair work to be completed and for any sum of damages and costs (not already paid) to be paid within that period. There is no reason why a tenant should not have further damages relating to the further period of discomfort and inconvenience, which can be easily worked out by reference to the original settlement sum. It may be of course that in certain circumstances the discomfort and inconvenience caused by the extended period of disrepair may warrant a higher sum of damages to be paid.

In an appropriate case, it could be argued that the tenant's human rights have been breached on the basis that it was *prima facie* a serious breach of the tenant's respect for their family life and home by the Defendant failing to carry out the repair work pursuant to its earlier agreement. Again, this should really be reserved for serious cases.

It is also suggested that it would be appropriate to seek aggravated damages in tort as well as further damages for discomfort and inconvenience in contract. Aggravated damages compensate a Claimant for injury to feelings. Such damages are not available in contract, but only in tort. Therefore, any pleading should incorporate a cause of action not only for breach of contract, but also in the tort of negligence for having failed and/or refused to carry out the works of repair in accordance with the terms of the settlement agreement. Damages for further discomfort and inconvenience may not be particularly substantial. Aggravated damages may be much more substantial, and therefore could be well worth pursuing.

If ultimately the letter of claim is ignored, or met with some explanation which does not stand up to scrutiny, then the tenant's remedy would be to issue fresh proceedings for breach of the settlement agreement.

It is suggested that the particulars of claim for breach of the settlement agreement would follow a standard pattern for a breach of contract case. It would plead the identity of the tenant in the contract and the address to which the claim relates, and the identity of the landlord, these being the contracting parties.

The pleading would then go on to describe the settlement agreement between the parties and set out the terms of that settlement. The actual agreement can then be referred to as, for example, "Annex 1" attached to the pleading. Any other relevant documents can also be annexed given the relevant numbering.

There can then be a description of what if anything was honoured in the agreement, and what was not. It is not unusual for example for damages and costs to have been paid, but only some of the works of repair to have been carried out, or even perhaps none at all.

If there were any further offers made in settlement following the landlord's breach, these can also be pleaded and annexed as appropriate.

Finally, the prayer to the pleading would in the usual way seek damages at the relevant level; an order for specific performance of the landlord's repairing obligation (or if appropriate damages in lieu); aggravated damages in tort; if appropriate to the case, a declaration that the tenant's human rights have been breached; and costs.

Further, and importantly, there is no reason why the tenant could not ask for a penal notice to be attached to any court order, as discussed above.

CHAPTER FOURTEEN

INSTRUCTING A SURVEYOR

Is an MRICS surveyor optional or essential?

It is suggested that a surveyor should at least have the qualification of being a Member of the Royal Institute of Chartered Surveyors (MRICS). Whilst some landlords do use MRICS surveyors, the overwhelming majority do not. They tend to use in-house employees who have various titles, for example "in-house surveyor"; "litigation surveyor"; or "contract works officer". Whilst these in-house employees may indeed have various qualifications, most do not have a degree and most are not MRICS qualified. The significance of this is that if, as is very often the case, there is a conflict of opinion between the Claimant's surveyor and the landlord's "surveyor" (to use the term loosely), then the tenant will want to be able to rely on his expert's superior qualification/s if it comes to a judge at the trial having to choose which of two competing opinions he prefers. That is not of course to say that an MRICS surveyor is always right, it's just that his qualification is likely to give him the edge in the opinion he expresses, and the approach of the judge to his evidence.

It is of course essential that any surveyor instructed is fully conversant with the context in which he is being given instructions i.e. that he understands that he is preparing a survey report for litigation purposes, and that it is not the same type of report that he might prepare for a potential purchaser of a house to live in, or on behalf of a bank or building society lending on a mortgage. A later chapter of this book is devoted to the role of a surveyor in housing conditions litigation, and all surveyors should become fully familiar with the contents of that chapter.

Solicitors should follow the requirements of the Protocol in relation to the instruction of surveyors which are set out at paragraphs 5.2 (h) and (i), and paragraphs 7.2 and 7.3. Paragraphs 7.4 to 7.8 of the Protocol deal further with experts. It goes without saying that any solicitor conducting this type of litigation (together with all ancillary staff) must become fully familiar and conversant with the Protocol requirements.

CHAPTER FIFTEEN

INSTRUCTING COUNSEL

If possible, instruct counsel by recommendation.

If that is not possible, then instruct chambers that profess to have a speciality in landlord and tenant work, especially in housing conditions work. However, some chambers specialise in defence work whereas others will predominantly if not exclusively represent tenants. You will need to instruct the latter. Counsel should be willing to enter into a Conditional Fee Agreement on the usual terms applicable between counsel and solicitor.

It is worth remembering however that when an area of law becomes popular and potentially lucrative, suddenly "experts" in that area pop up out of the woodwork in numerous barristers chambers. Caution needs to be exercised, as these self-styled experts may well lack the necessary expertise to provide the sort of services upon which an instructing solicitor needs to rely.

The overwhelming majority of solicitors have long ago recognised that the Bar has a lot to offer as part of the litigation process. Their expertise is different to that of solicitors. Essentially their expertise relates to advising on liability, evidence and quantum of damages; drafting pleadings; and performing the duties of an advocate at court for any applications, case management conferences, trials, and appeals. It is suggested that as a general rule it would be a false economy to have solicitors, legal executives, or inexperienced junior staff attempting to perform the traditional roles of counsel, as the skill set of counsel is learned over a number of years and after having had the benefit of pupillage with a senior barrister.

The fee earners in a solicitor's office have more than enough to do in managing their own caseload. Most solicitors will readily appreciate that instructing their own fee earners to perform the tasks traditionally carried out by counsel is unwise and often leads to problems, which in turn, in the context of litigation, can turn out to be expensive. Ideally, housing conditions cases need to be run quickly and smoothly towards their conclusion with as few mistakes as possible. Experience has shown that the relationship of fee earners and counsel working together is a successful formula which has worked for generations.

Having been through the various preparatory stages discussed above, it would be advisable to instruct counsel for a conference with the tenant. This should be done sooner rather than later. Do not let a potential personal injury cause of action delay instructing counsel, as this potential claim can be investigated concurrently, and any proceedings which are issued can always be amended in due course to include the personal injury claim if causation can be established. Any pleading by counsel in the housing conditions claim would usually make reference to the fact that a personal injury claim is being investigated and that an amendment to the pleading will be made in due course if causation is established.

There is no reason why a conference with Counsel cannot be by telephone with the tenant. These need not be lengthy, and experience has shown that 20 to 30 minutes would suffice. A difficult case may take longer. If counsel has a pre-prepared conference agenda there is no reason why the conference cannot be conducted in a relatively short period of time by means of a series of questions and answers following that agenda. Many conferences will follow the same pattern, as the same essential information is required from each tenant in each case. Counsel will then have all the information he needs to draft the pleading if appropriate.

It would be helpful for tenants in any case to compile their own schedule of special damages which the solicitor can ask them to do at any time either before or after instructing counsel. This saves time in the conference and makes for a much more accurate special damages claim.

If this exercise is done during the conference items may be missed or forgotten due to the pressure of time.

It should be made clear to any Counsel instructed that as a general rule a turnaround of papers of no more than 7 days is expected. Housing conditions cases are often serious with tenants living in poor, or very poor conditions, with a personal injury element not being uncommon. Delays by counsel (and surveyors) should be very much the exception rather than the rule. Tenants are often desperate by the time they instruct a solicitor and do not expect unwarranted delays in the legal services provided.

Tenants should be telephoned and/or emailed and/or sent a text message a week before the conference, and the day before the conference (or even on the day of the conference) to ensure that they attend and don't forget that it has been arranged. As everyone knows, is commonly done and works well for medical and dental appointments, and it will work well for conference appointments in housing conditions cases.

PART TWO

COUNSEL

CHAPTER SIXTEEN

THE ROLE OF COUNSEL

When counsel receives his instructions from his instructing solicitor, his first job after reading them will be to organise a conference (almost always by telephone) with the tenant. The arrangements for a conference are essentially a personal matter between counsel, solicitor and tenant, but experience has shown that telephone conferences work well. Each counsel will have his own idea as to what essential information he feels is necessary to obtain from the client in order to draft an effective pleading.

As an aside, a fairly rigid agenda is helpful because tenants will often talk in a very unstructured manner about their problems and experiences in the house in question, and it is easy for them to go off on tangents – usually because of the frustration they feel at the inactivity of the landlord in relation to the disrepair problems. This can then lead to their discussions about the complete absence of repair work, shoddy workmanship, missed appointments by the landlord's workmen, illness, ruined property, and generally being fobbed off. Whilst all of these matters are important, the time taken to elicit the important information is significantly shortened if the conference is conducted generally by means of questions and answers in an ordered fashion. This assists both counsel and the tenant.

The particulars of claim

Pleadings are personal to counsel, and as long as they comply with the requirements of CPR Part 16, the style and contents of the pleading are entirely a matter for the discretion of counsel drafting them. Each particulars of claim is of course a unique document and sensitive to the facts of the particular case. The following is a guide as to what must be included in a statement of case for a housing conditions claim:

1. The relationship between the Claimant and the Defendant i.e. that the Claimant is the tenant and the Defendant is the landlord of the dwelling house to which the claim relates, and its address. It would be helpful to include the date on which the tenancy commenced, the ages of all occupants and their relationship to the tenant, and the rent paid.

2. The various causes of action appropriate to the case. The following should be considered for inclusion: the implied repairing obligation pursuant to section 11 of the Landlord and Tenant Act 1985; unfitness for human habitation pursuant to sections 9A to 10 of the 1985 Act; section 4 of the Defective Premises Act 1972.

3. Any cause of action involving Human Rights and which if any rights have been breached – discussed elsewhere in this book.

4. The express repairing obligation contained in the tenancy agreement.

5. Any alleged breach of the implied or express repairing obligations should be pleaded, followed by details of notice of disrepair/unfit housing conditions given by the tenant to the landlord; the date or dates on which notice was given to the best of the tenant's recollection. If precision is not possible from the tenant (and often it isn't), they should at least attempt to be as accurate as possible as to the first date on which notice was given, even if this relates only to the year in question.

   The date or dates of notice given to the landlord is not always easy to plead, as many tenants do not keep accurate records, and are much more likely to remember when they <u>first</u> gave notice, and roughly how many times they gave it thereafter about any particular item of disrepair. Those tenants who have kept a record of emails sent to their landlord and any other documentation of any sort which can corroborate their case on notice should be carefully retained and if possible copied to their solicitor. Each individual item of disrepair about which notice was given should be pleaded.

6. If the landlord's disclosed repair records show any or all of the alleged notice given, this should be pleaded, giving some detail as to dates and the subject matter of the complaint.

7. Assuming that a surveyor's report has been obtained on behalf of the tenant, the identity of the surveyor and his report should be pleaded, and his report should be annexed to the pleading. So too, strictly speaking, should the tenancy agreement, if this is available.

8. All other examples of notice given by the tenant to the landlord should be pleaded including any correspondence from any source, such as MPs, councillors, GPs, social workers etc. in addition of course to the solicitor's Protocol letter of claim.

9. Because breach of the repairing obligation is a continuing cause of action, it renews daily until or repair work is satisfactorily completed – see *Grenada Theatres Ltd v Freehold Investments (Leytonstone) Ltd [1959] Ch 592 at page 608*. Accordingly if the landlord has had more than a reasonable amount of time to carry out repair work following receipt of the letter of claim then it is arguably in breach of its repairing obligation, at very least from a date which could be said to be a reasonable amount of time following service of that letter. What would be a reasonable amount of time? A good indication would come from the landlord's own documentation as to its timescales for carrying out urgent repairs, non-urgent repairs and routine repairs. If not contained in the landlord's tenancy conditions, this information can sometimes be found on the landlord's website.

10. The same can be said in relation to what if any work has been carried out following receipt of the surveyor's report – either single, joint, or single joint expert report. The tenant's case of course is predicated upon notice given personally by him or on his behalf to the landlord. It is suggested however that even if the tenant's evidence on notice was ultimately not accepted, he may still have a viable cause of action due to the landlord's inactivity in relation to repair work following receipt of the letter of claim and/or the expert evidence – because it is a continuing cause of action – but this would have to be pleaded.

11. The next part of the pleading should cover the ways in which the tenant's use and occupation of the dwelling house has been affected by the landlord's breach of covenant, setting out particulars of discomfort and inconvenience. This may of course include any allegations of personal injury to the tenant and/or any of the other occupants.

12. Details of any personal injury claims should be pleaded giving all the usual details and any medical evidence upon which reliance is placed. If there is no medical evidence yet available, the pleading can simply say that evidence is being collated in relation to a particular personal injury claim and that the pleading will be amended in due course if causation is established.

    It is suggested that this is an appropriate way of dealing with the subject of personal injury as it would be inappropriate to delay issue of proceedings pending what may be weeks or even months of collating the necessary evidence to support the personal injury claim.

13. If there is a claim for personal injury and or loss of property, then breach of section 4 of the Defective Premises Act 1972 needs to be pleaded. This provision gives a right of action in tort in what essentially is a contractual claim.

14. Particulars of special damages. If they are few in number, they can simply be put in the pleading. If more complicated, then it would probably best be dealt with in a schedule of loss which can be annexed to the pleading.

    Apart from the obvious losses, consideration should be given to the less obvious ones like: additional heating expenses in a bad damp or draughty windows case; loss of earnings caused for example by inability to work due to personal injury, lost wages due to taking time off work for appointments which the landlord's servants or agents failed to keep for no apparent reason – which is surprisingly often.

15. Unfitness for human habitation if appropriate, and the basis upon which the cause of action is alleged.

The above matters are the essentials of a statement of case and form the basis of a proper pleading in a housing conditions case, and any ancillary causes of action discussed above. The pleading must always of course comply with the Civil Procedure Rules in relation to the contents of the particulars of claim as set out in CPR 16.4.

The following are matters which counsel may at his discretion feel are ancillary matters, but nevertheless important and appropriate to plead in the statement of case:

1. The reasons why the Claimant chose to litigate – e.g. denial of liability; a failure either to admit or deny liability; in order to promote the speedy and appropriate carrying out of repair work; in order to obtain compensation relating to one or more causes of action.

2. Any failures to comply with the Housing Conditions Protocol – e.g. failing to instruct an expert in accordance with paragraphs 7.2 and 7.3 of the Protocol; failing to admit or deny liability;

failing to provide a schedule of repair work in compliance with paragraph 6.3 (d) of the Protocol.

3. Reference can be made if appropriate to the case of *DSN v Blackpool Football Club Ltd (Rev 1) (2020) EWHC 670 (QB) (Indemnity Costs),* in particular within paragraph 28, which states that *"no defence, however strong, justifies a failure to engage in any kind of alternative dispute resolution".*

4. Any findings of maladministration against the landlord in question by the Housing Ombudsman Service, which are available to view as a public document on the Ombudsman's website. Defendants often question how this is relevant. It is suggested that its relevance lies in the fact that findings of maladministration give an indication as to the landlord's general attitude to its housing management function, and an indication specifically in relation to the particular Claimant.

5. In any case where the landlord is alleging that the damp and mould problems are as a result of the tenant's lifestyle, it may be relevant in appropriate cases to make reference to the report of the Housing Ombudsman Service dated 26 October 2021 entitled: "Spotlight on Damp and Mould" in which it is said:

   > *"Our investigation heard immense frustration and sense of unfairness at the information sometimes provided to residents about issues like condensation. This occurred so often it is appropriate to call it systemic. The word "lifestyle", when it may be a consequence of limited choices, should be banished from the vernacular".*

6. Counsel may also feel it appropriate to plead a formal request for disclosure of the evidence which has been provided to the Ombudsman following his request for evidence of:

a) its approach to assessing the extent of damp and mould issues in its homes;

b) its most recent assessment of the extent of damp and mould hazards;

c) the action it is taking to remedy them; and

d) the process it has to identify and deal promptly with damp and mould cases when they are raised by tenants.

All of the above refers to counsel being instructed to deal with pleadings (rather than the fee earner having conduct of the case) as the vast majority of solicitors firms will prefer pleadings to be drafted by counsel rather than done in-house. The contents of the pleading may of course change from time to time not only to suit the particular facts of a case, but also to take into account the fact that statute law and case law continue to develop. For example, fitness for human habitation now has to be considered in many cases following the new sections 9A-10 of the 1985 Act.

Defendants may (and frequently do) object to the style and/or content of the pleading, but many of these objections can be dealt with in a Reply to the defence. No one can claim infallibility in relation to the correctness or otherwise of a pleading and ultimately the contents must lie with counsel's discretion. If something included in a pleading is accepted as being manifestly wrong or inappropriate, it can be acknowledged in a Reply as wrong and the mistake should not be repeated in any future pleadings.

One of the documents which should always be part of counsel's instructions, if it is available, is the tenancy agreement. It should always be obtained from the Defendant by way of disclosure. If not disclosed in response to the letter of claim, a Subject Access Request should be made for it (and any other missing disclosable documents). The document is important not only in helping to determine the identity of the correct Defendant, but also to ascertain the actual wording of the express repairing covenant in the lease.

Most tenancy agreements refer to the landlord's obligation to keep in repair the structure and exterior of the tenant's *home* or *the property* or *the premises*. It should be understood that these are all much bigger concepts than *the dwelling house* which is the wording used in s.11 of the 1985 Act. The structure and exterior of the dwelling house is literally the 4 walls and everything structural inside them. *Home* and *property* and *premises* encompass, it is suggested, fences, walls, gates, outhouses etc which are all part of the tenant's *home etc*. Landlords often use even "looser" expressions when defining the scope of their repairing obligation – see *Welsh v Greenwich LBC [2000] 6 WLUK 716*. All these words and phrases significantly help the tenant's case. That is why it is important to check the wording of the tenancy agreement and to make it available to counsel prior to him drafting the particulars of claim.

<u>The Reply (and defence to counterclaim)</u>

A Reply to the defence will be necessary in the majority of cases, if not all cases where a defence is filed. Landlords often believe they have good points in their defence which, when carefully analysed have little if any substance. As with any litigation, pleadings are designed to ensure the parties know the case they have to meet. It is not uncommon for a Defendant to start thinking in terms of settlement once the Reply has been served. Again, it is important to ensure that the Reply is both correct and effective, and it's drafting should be left to counsel.

<u>What points need to to be considered in a Reply?</u>

Each of the following matters, if raised, needs to be considered carefully and responded to if necessary.

The common defences are:

a. The item complained of does not fall within the repairing obligation;

b. The landlord has never had notice of the disrepair prior to the letter of claim;

c. The landlord has had notice of it in the past but carried out repair works with no further complaint thereafter;

d. The tenant failed (continually) to provide access for repair work to be carried out;

e. The item in question is not in disrepair, or it is *de minimis*;

f. The particulars of notice given in the particulars of claim are inadequate and insufficient to enable the Defendant to know the case it has to meet.

Dealing with each of these items in turn:

a. The repairing obligation. Whether or not an item of alleged disrepair is in fact an item falling within the landlord's implied or express repairing obligation is a matter of law, or arguably, mixed law and fact. Although surveyors often express an opinion, they are not lawyers and (with respect to them) their opinion usually carries little weight in this regard. Their function is simply to express a professional opinion as to whether disrepair exists in any given situation (as defined by the case law – see *Quick v Taff Ely Borough Council [1986] 1 QB 809*). Arguably they should express an opinion as to whether or not a dwelling is unfit for human habitation, and if such an opinion is expressed, this could be one factor which a judge would be entitled to take into account in deciding whether in his judgement the dwelling is indeed unfit for human habitation.

b. Denial of notice. This is a common defence, but conceptually is problematic for the landlord. As a matter of common sense it would be rare (although not impossible) for a tenant to sit in poor housing conditions without making a complaint. This is especially so if the disrepair involves damp, drafts, a defective heating installation, a defective or dangerous electrical installation, unsightliness, inability to decorate, embarrassment to have visitors, illness being caused by the disrepair, etc. Telephone records if available and copy emails are always of course helpful to support a tenant's case. Tenants who have a pay-as-you-go mobile phone will not have access to records. It is always worth asking a tenant therefore if this is the type of mobile phone which they have, as the landlord can be informed either in correspondence or in a pleading that telephone records are not available in support of the tenant's contentions about notice.

c. The landlord has carried out repair work already. Shoddy repair work and botched jobs do not fulfil the repairing obligation – see the case law cited by Luba et al. – in particular *Elmcroft Developments v Tankersley-Sawyer 270 EG 140 (CA).*

d. "Failed" access. This is a phrase often used by landlords in their defence. Similar phrases are often deployed, but the "no access" defence is often lacking in substance. This is because the landlord has defined duties in relation to access which, unless those duties complied with, could not be relied upon by the landlord as a defence.

It will be seen from section 11(6) of the 1985 Act that a tenant is required to permit access to the landlord in accordance with the obligation imposed on the tenant by the tenancy agreement (and indeed by statute) only if the landlord has first given at least 24 hours prior *written* notice.

It is also important to check whether the terms of the tenancy agreement require the landlord to give written notice to the tenant before exercising its right of entry. Emergencies would be excepted in all cases.

As regards the common law duty, again the dicta in *Grenada Theatres Ltd v Freehold Investments (Leytonstone) Ltd [1959] Ch 592 at page 608* are relevant.

e. The item in question is not in disrepair. This of course will be a question of degree in every case and is entirely fact sensitive. However, as a matter of law, disrepair which is truly trivial will not as a general rule fall within the landlord's repairing obligation. As mentioned above, whether or not something is in disrepair is a matter of law, or mixed law and fact, applying the test laid down by the case law – i.e. is the item in question in a worse condition than it was at some earlier time. Subject to the *de minimis* rule, it is this that should be the determining factor when a judge decides on this point.

f. The particulars of notice given are inadequate and insufficient to enable the Defendant to know the case that it has to meet. This is not so much a defence, although often raised in the defence, and again more often than not lacks substance. There is a useful and important passage in the judgement of the Court of Appeal in the case of *Uddin and another v Islington London Borough Council [2015] EWCA Civ 369.* Although it is lengthy, it is extremely useful to deploy it in a Reply. Lewison LJ at paragraph 25 of his judgement said the following:

> "*the next ground of appeal is that the particulars of claim did not plead a defective damp proof course. That is quite correct. They did not. The question is what, if any, consequences flow from that. As Saville LJ pointed out in British Airways Pension Trustees Ltd v Sir Robert McAlpine and Sons Ltd [1994] 45 Con LR 81*:
>
> *"The basic purpose of pleadings is to enable the opposing party to know what case is being made in sufficient detail to enable that party properly to prepare to answer it. To my mind, it seems that in recent years there has been a tendency to forget this basic purpose and to seek particularisation even when it is not really required. This is not only costly in itself, but is calculated to lead to delay*

> *and to interlocutory battles in which the parties and the court pore over endless pages of pleadings to see whether or not some particular point has or has not been raised or answered when in truth each party knows perfectly well what case is being made by the other and is able properly to prepare to deal with it. Pleadings are not a game to be played at the expense of litigants, nor an end in themselves, but a means to the end and that end is to give each party a fair hearing."*

At paragraph 26 of his judgement he then said:

> *"Much the same points were made by Lord Woolf MR in McPhilemy v Times Newspapers Ltd [1999] 3 All ER 775 at 792.*

At paragraph 31 of his judgement he then said:

> *"Had Islington been in any doubt about the case that it was preparing to meet, it could have made a request for further information, but it never did."*

It should be remembered that failures either by the Claimant or the Defendant to comply with the requirements of the Housing Conditions Protocol does not negate a claim or defence, but could ultimately give rise to some extent to an adverse costs order.

CHAPTER SEVENTEEN

OTHER POINTS COMMONLY RAISED IN THE DEFENCE

Often a landlord denies failing to comply with its Protocol obligations. In these circumstances it would be appropriate in the Reply to ask the landlord to provide details of all documentation that it has in its possession evidencing its denial. It can be pointed out in the pleading that if the landlord fails to disclose that documentation, then the court at the trial will be invited to draw the obvious conclusion from that failure.

Another matter frequently raised is the defence available to the landlord under section 11 (2) of the 1985 Act – i.e. that the disrepair alleged has been caused by the tenant (or anyone for whom the tenant is responsible). It is pertinent to point out in the Reply that the burden of proving such an allegation would rest firmly with the landlord. There is no burden of proof on the tenant to negate such an allegation.

The same can be said in relation to the landlord's frequent claim in the defence that the dampness in the dwelling house is condensation related and not caused by any defects in the structure or exterior. Whilst this is an easy allegation to make, the burden of proving it will rest on the landlord. He who asserts must prove.

Where however the tenant acknowledges that there is condensation dampness, and concomitant mould, the burden of proving that the dampness is <u>uncontrollable</u> despite every normal precaution taken to prevent it, the burden of proof on that issue, it is suggested, would rest on the tenant. The tenant's surveyor's evidence would be key in proving this point. The surveyor would have to consider all possible causes of condensation before expressing an opinion as to whether or not it is the tenant's use and occupation of the premises which is responsible for the condensation and mould problem, or conversely, whether the cause is beyond the tenant's control. If the latter, the surveyor should explain (and be instructed to explain) why this is so.

One or two other points which often arise in defences are the following:

Is the person who has signed the statement of truth on behalf of a company or corporation entitled to sign it, bearing in mind CPR PD 22 3.4 and 3.5?

Rule 3.4 states that where a document is to be verified on behalf of a company or other corporation, then subject to paragraph 3.7, the statement of truth must be signed by a person holding a senior position in the company or corporation. Paragraph 6.2 of PD 6A sets out the meaning of "senior position".

Rule 3.5 states that each of the following persons is a person holding a senior position – (1) in respect of a registered company or corporation, a director, the treasurer, secretary, chief executive, manager or other officer of the company or corporation, and (2) in respect of a corporation which is not a registered company, in addition to those persons set out in (1), the mayor, chairman, president or town clerk or other similar officer of the corporation.

If the statement of truth has not been signed by any of the above, the statement is invalid and Rule 22.2 will apply.

Counterclaims

Is the counterclaim admitted nor denied? This should be dealt with as appropriate. If the counterclaim is denied, the relevant requirements are set out in CPR 16.5

A common counterclaim by a landlord is that the tenant owes a certain sum in rent arrears. The payment of rent is an obligation arising by virtue of the tenancy agreement, which of course is a contract, and therefore the limitation period in relation to contract will apply. Accordingly any rent arrears which have accrued more than 6 years prior to the date of the counterclaim will be statute barred by effluxion of time, and this should be pleaded in the defence to the counterclaim. The burden of proof will then fall to the landlord to demonstrate that none of the alleged arrears are statute barred.

If the tenant does not know whether he is in arrears or, if he is in arrears what that exact sum is, then this should be neither admitted nor denied but should be a matter which the landlord is required to prove.

CHAPTER EIGHTEEN

ALLOCATION HEARINGS

Those representing both tenants and landlords will realise that the track to which a claim is allocated is an important matter. Generally tenants contend for a fast-track allocation or occasionally, if appropriate, a multitrack allocation. Conversely, landlords whenever possible contend for allocation to the small claims track. The ramifications in relation to costs in both scenarios are obvious.

The relevant rules governing allocation to track are to be found at CPR 26.5 to 26.8. The relevant rule in housing conditions claims is rule 26.6 (1) (b).

It is important to notice that the small claims track is only the normal track for any claim which includes a claim by a tenant of residential premises against the landlord where the cost of the repairs or other work to the premises is estimated to be not more than £1000 and the value of any other claim for damages is not more than £1000. In other words, both of these elements are required before a case is suitable for small claims track allocation.

The note in the White Book at 26.6.3 make the effect of the rule clear. The note states that if there is a claim for both damages and an order for works to be carried out the case will not be allocated to the small claims track if either the cost of the works or the damages claim is more than £1000. In such circumstances the case will normally be allocated to the fast-track, unless the financial value of the claim is more than the value fixed by rule 26.6 (4) (b). Claims for both damages and an order for works to be carried out will only be allocated to the small claims track if the cost of the work is less than £1000 and the claim for damages is less than £1000. That interpretation is borne out by PD 7A para 3.

Those conducting allocation hearings should be familiar with that rule and the White Book commentary.

If it is clear that all works have been satisfactorily completed, then prima facie the case will be allocated to the small claims track unless the value of general and special damages combined exceeds £10,000.

It is therefore of the utmost importance that the fee earner having conduct of the case contacts the tenant shortly before any allocation hearing to ascertain what if any works of repair have been carried out by the landlord, and what remain outstanding. If any actionable disrepair work remains outstanding then the fee earner should take careful instructions from the tenant, and then compile a short witness statement setting out clearly the position, signed of course with a statement of truth. The witness statement can be that of the fee earner and need not be that of the tenant, especially if time is short. This will inevitably be a document of great importance in any arguments about allocation to track and therefore must be filed at court and served on the Defendant in the days leading up to the court hearing.

Even if all of repair work has been satisfactorily carried out, the matters set out at CPR 26.8 may still be relevant to the question of allocation to track.

Some or all of the following arguments may be advanced:

i. If the Defendant is contending that all works of repair are now satisfactorily complete, where is its evidence of that fact? Why has the Defendant not filed and served a witness statement to that effect, especially if the Claimant has filed and served one contending that repairs are not complete?

ii. Again, if the Defendant is contending that all works of repair are complete, why hasn't it made an application for summary judgement in relation to the claim for specific performance? The Defendant at an allocation hearing would *effectively* be asking for summary judgement on the claim for specific performance without any formal application being made and possibly without any evidence supporting the contention.

iii. There is no provision in the small claims track for asking questions of the experts. The maximum sum payable (at the moment) to an expert is £750 including VAT. How therefore is an expert to be paid if the Claimant wants to ask questions under CPR Part 35?

iv. If the court orders a joint statement of experts because the experts are not in agreement with each other, again how are the experts to be paid?

v. By the allocation stage, there has been no order for disclosure. It is conceivable that an unscrupulous Defendant could hide documents from the Claimant which should be disclosed. However in the small claims track the parties do not have to sign a disclosure statement with a statement of truth.

It should be noted following the guidance given by the Court of Appeal in the case cited in the next section (Birmingham v Lee) the correct costs order at the conclusion of any allocation hearing is costs in the case.

CHAPTER NINETEEN

BIRMINGHAM CITY COUNCIL V AVRIL LEE [2008] EWCA CIV 891

Unfortunately there is much confusion over the effect of the Court of Appeal's judgement in this case.

Paragraph 11 of the Housing Conditions Protocol says this: "if the tenant's claim is settled without litigation on terms which justify bringing it, the landlord will pay the tenant's reasonable costs....".

Whilst in theory this might apply to a situation before a tenant has consulted solicitors, the reality is that the judgement in *Birmingham v Lee* will come into effect in two basic situations.

First, if following the letter of claim, a settlement is reached between the parties either by means of a compromise agreement or the making of a Part 36 offer which is accepted, then the tenant will be entitled to his costs on the standard basis in accordance with the usual principles and in accordance with paragraph 11 of the Protocol just cited. If the matter is settled pursuant to a Part 36 offer and acceptance, then of course the tenant is entitled to his costs under CPR 36.13 (1). If settled pursuant to a compromise agreement, the tenant is entitled to his costs only by agreement between the parties – i.e. the compromise includes a provision for the landlord to pay the tenant's costs. The only exception is that if the claim is and was always a small claim which would only ever be heard on the small claims track – i.e. the claim for damages and the cost of repair work are agreed by the parties to be both under £1000 – see CPR 26.6 (1) (b), then the tenant would only be entitled to the costs which are allowable on the small claims track in accordance with CPR Part 27.

Secondly, if following the issue of proceedings, all of the repair work is carried out by the landlord to the appropriate standard, the tenant will still be entitled to his costs up to the date that the repair work is completed. There is however an important caveat to that. The tenant is only entitled to his costs if he goes on to win the case, or alternatively the case is settled before trial with the landlord agreeing to pay the Claimant's costs (as a commercial decision) without having to bear the risk of losing at trial, and having to pay its own costs, even if it wins. Obviously if the landlord intends to settle on a commercial basis then it would be in its interests to do so sooner rather than later.

Hence the usual battleground over allocation, because the losing landlord's costs liability to the successful tenant will obviously be much higher if the case is allocated to the fast track, given that there are no costs payable by either side following allocation to the small claims track (save those payable for unreasonable behaviour under CPR 27.14 (2) (g)).

There is a part of the judgement in the *Birmingham v Lee* which is worth citing at paragraphs 33 and 34:

> *"Since the promulgation of the Protocol it is no longer the case that a claim is only made (for costs purposes at least) when and if litigation is begun. On the contrary, the protocol requires a claim to be advanced initially in accordance with its terms, under a warning that there is likely to be a costs penalty if it is not. The references to costs which are contained in the protocol, and which we have set out at paragraph 15 above, clearly demonstrate that the object of the protocol is to achieve settlement of disrepair claims without recourse to litigation. Its object is very clearly that, provided the claim was justified, it ought to be settled on terms which include the payment of the tenant's reasonable costs: and costs calculated according to the track which the claim would fall to if made by way of litigation.*
>
> *Without some order as to the early-incurred costs, it would be open to a landlord who is in fact and in law liable for want of repairs to adopt a deliberate policy of omitting to repair until the Protocol letter is*

received, but then of repairing without admission of liability so as to ensure that any subsequent court claim fell to the small claims track. The result of that would be that fast track costs which would otherwise have been due to the tenant would no longer be payable. We do not say that this is what has happened here; it may well not be. But that very possible scenario illustrates the necessity for some order in relation to the costs of advancing the protocol claim. Moreover, quite independently of the possibility of any such deliberate manipulation of the process by a landlord, such an order is necessary if the protocol is not to operate as a means of preventing recovery of reasonably incurred costs. The tenant who has a justifiable claim for disrepair needs legal assistance in advancing it. He must initiate it in accordance with the Protocol. If the effect of the claim is to get the work done, then providing that the landlord was liable for the disrepair the tenant ought to recover the reasonable costs of achieving that result."

CHAPTER TWENTY

DAMAGES

General damages

The subject is dealt with in depth by Luba et al. to which, as always, the reader is referred. It is intended here only to give a basic overview so that the reader can calculate on a fairly broad brush basis what general damages in a case may be worth. There will be exceptions and the case law deals with unusual types of case, but the overwhelming majority of cases can happily be dealt with using the now well-known method propounded by the Court of Appeal in the case of *Wallace v Manchester City Council [1998] 7 WLUK 110* after reviewing many of the earlier decisions.

Essentially damages for discomfort and inconvenience are calculated by multiplying together two key figures. The first figure is the diminution in rental value. The second figure is the notice period.

There is no magic formula in arriving at an opinion on the diminution in rental value. It is essentially a matter of judgement and experience. To that extent, it might be said to be more of an art than a science. In simple terms, if the rent for a dwelling house is £100 a week, but given its state of disrepair and any other factors thought to have relevance, it is thought to be worth only £80 per week, then there is a diminution in rental value of 20%. Diminution in rental value is obviously a sliding scale. It is unlikely, but certainly possible, that minor cases will attract a diminution in rental value of 10% or possibly even less. It is suggested that most cases fall in the bracket of 10% to 30%, but serious cases can obviously be higher, and there is authority at County Court level that if a dwelling is uninhabitable, the diminution in rental value should be 100% – see *Whittington v Uddin December 2014 Legal Action 28.* It is submitted that this accords entirely with common sense.

Having formed a view of the appropriate diminution in rental value, consideration then has to be given to the notice period i.e. for how long has the tenant been reporting the disrepair to the landlord and the disrepair has not been remedied? This figure can sometimes be ascertained from the landlord's records, which unfortunately are not always reliable (although nearly all landlords would say otherwise). More often it will be ascertained from the tenant to the best of the tenant's ability and recollection.

Some tenants actually keep records of complaints, and they have paperwork and emails to substantiate their contentions about notice. Every effort should be made to obtain such evidence from the tenant as this is likely to prove to be important at some point in the future. It is also disclosable information by the tenant.

The Housing Ombudsman is shortly to commence a formal review of landlord's record keeping and data management, due to the fact that more than two thirds of the Ombudsman's determinations with a finding of maladministration identified record-keeping as an issue. In his press release of 8 November 2022 the Ombudsman called for evidence to support his next systemic investigation.

Having given that background, it would be useful to look at a simple example.

Having decided that the appropriate diminution in rental value is 20% against an annual rent of £5200 (£100 per week) and taking a notice period for the purposes of this example of 4 years, the calculation would be as follows:

£5200 x 20% (diminution in rental value) = £1040 x 4 (notice period) = £4160

on the assumption that the case is being funded by a conditional fee agreement, 10% can be added to that figure to take account of the rule in *Simmons v Castle [2012] EWCA Civ 1288* (which applies to housing conditions cases) producing a final figure of general damages of £4576.

Aggravating and mitigating features which inform the level of damages

Each case will of course be unique on its own facts, but it might be said that a young single man living on his own is rather different than a young unmarried mother struggling to cope with 2 or 3 children at home, or an elderly disabled person who spends much of his or her time at home. Whilst they all may be inconvenienced or even upset at the discomfort caused by the state of disrepair of their home, the young single man may be out at work all day and, possibly, may go out several nights a week as well. This is unlikely to be the lifestyle of the young mother, who may spend a lot more time at home, and also worries for the health and safety of her children. The permutations of course are endless.

It is suggested that (as part of the broad-brush process) the case of the young man may to some extent mitigate the level of damages, whereas in the other 2 cases there would be a valid argument for an increase in the level of their damages because the discomfort, upset and inconvenience is arguably that much more. However ultimately, as stated above, each case will turn on its own facts, but it is submitted that these are relevant matters for consideration.

Special damages

It is suggested that if there are only one or 2 straightforward items, there is no reason why these cannot simply be included in the particulars of claim under the heading "special damages".

If not included in this way, then they should be set out in a document entitled "schedule of loss" which should then be annexed to the particulars of claim.

There will be the obvious items which fall under this head of damages which need little discussion – e.g. ruined wallpaper/paint, carpets, curtains, blinds, laminate flooring, clothing and footwear, beds, bedding etc. The list in theory could be endless.

Less commonly considered are, for example, additional heating expenses which are often relevant in draughty window cases, and sometimes in damp cases also, as tenants often complain that regardless of the amount of heat they use, they can never heat their home to a reasonable ambient temperature because of damp.

How is this figure to be calculated? In the absence of a comparison of heating bills across various periods of time, which is unlikely to be a viable exercise for a variety of different reasons, it is suggested that a reasonable average figure should be pleaded for additional heating expenditure, which should be confirmed as being reasonable by the tenant. For example, an additional £10 per week for the 6 cold months of the year (some might say 7 or 8 cold months depending on geographical location), multiplied by the number of years for which the additional heating has been required.

A paragraph can then be added to the particulars of special damages/schedule of loss, for example:

> "*It is averred for the avoidance of doubt that estimating the cost of additional heating is entirely appropriate in the context of a fast track case, as opposed to incurring the very considerable expense of instructing an expert to prepare a report incorporating scientific calculations*".

Another item worth considering that many tenants forget to mention, but should be asked about, is whether they spend additional sums on cleaning materials to deal with removal of mould, and also whether they use air fresheners (either plug-in or sprays), scented candles or scented sticks to mask the smell of damp in their home. This can often amount to a considerable sum of money over time, and is worth including in a schedule of special damages.

As mentioned above, the permutations are virtually endless, but one final head of loss to consider is that many tenants complain that they have taken time off work specifically for an inspection, or for repair work to be carried out, and no one from the landlord or the landlord's agents turns up to keep the appointment without explanation or apology. In addition to being angry and frustrated at this situation, some of these tenants will have lost one or more days' wages as a result. Subject to appropriate proof, these lost wages are a valid head of loss, and accordingly should be claimed.

Finally, it should be remembered that for allocation purposes CPR 26.6 (1) (b) (iii) speaks of the value of "any other claim for damages". Accordingly this will encompass a combination of general damages *and* special damages, and may well be a relevant consideration for the purposes of allocation.

PART THREE

SURVEYORS

CHAPTER TWENTY-ONE

THE FUNCTION OF THE SURVEYOR IN HOUSING CONDITIONS CASES

Whilst surveyors are trained professionals, they must appreciate that a survey in a housing conditions case is very different from a survey when carried out on behalf of a potential purchaser of property or a mortgagee. It is a survey and report for the purposes of litigation for alleged breach of repairing obligations. It is also a survey to consider whether in all the circumstances the dwelling is unfit for human habitation.

Relevant considerations

The first and probably the most important matter to consider is whether any part of the dwelling house is in disrepair. Disrepair is a question of fact, and has been defined in law as occurring *"when there is deterioration, i.e. when part of the building is in a worse condition than it was at some earlier time"*– see *Post Office v Aquarius Properties Ltd [1987] 1 All ER 1055* and *Quick v Taff Ely Borough Council [1986] 1 QB 809*. This common law definition should be a useful guide for surveyors when conducting their survey. It should however be remembered that any disrepair which is *de minimis* would not be actionable, and this should be said in the report.

The second matter for consideration is whether the dwelling is unfit for human habitation. Primarily this is a question of fact for the trial judge after hearing all of the evidence. However, the opinion of the surveyor may well be an important factor in the decision-making process, even if not definitive.

It will be necessary therefore for the surveyor to have a reasonable working knowledge of sections 9A, 10 and 11 of the 1985 Act and all surveyors should familiarise themselves with these statutory provisions.

Primarily a surveyor must deal with the items of alleged disrepair set out in the letter of claim which will have been sent to him as part of his instructions. However surveyors are also required by paragraph 7.1 (d) of the Pre-Action Protocol to report on all items of disrepair which the landlord ought reasonably to know about, or which the surveyor as the expert ought reasonably to report on.

It should be borne in mind that section 11(3) of the 1985 Act states that in determining the standard of repair required by the lessor's repairing covenant, regard shall be had to the age, character of the dwelling house and the locality in which it is situated. It is suggested however that all repairs must be to a good and workmanlike standard, using good and proper materials. Botched jobs or "sticking plaster" repairs would never be acceptable.

Long survey reports are unnecessary. Whilst it is ultimately a matter of style, it is not necessary, for example, to set out the statutory provisions of sections 9A, 10 and 11 of the 1985 Act in full. It would be sufficient merely to say that the surveyor is familiar with those particular sections and that they have been borne in mind in the preparation of the survey report.

The language of a report

Surveyors should be careful when using the word "structural". Often surveyors say that there is no structural disrepair. Almost invariably the surveyor means that he has found no disrepair affecting the *structural integrity* of the building. However, the word structural has a wider meaning in law than disrepair affecting only the structural integrity of the building. The most obvious and common item of the structure which is affected by disrepair is the plasterwork on the interior walls. The Court of Appeal in the case of *Grand v Gill [2011] EWCA CIV 554* ruled that interior plasterwork is part of the structure of the dwelling house. Accordingly, it would be wrong to say that there are no structural defects in a dwelling house if there is disrepair to the interior plasterwork.

Surveyors should not use words in a report such as "possibly", "may", "might" and similar expressions. These words imply *possibility* not *probability* and are generally inappropriate in the context of litigation. The burden of proving disrepair lies upon the tenant. The standard of proof is on the balance of probabilities, or to put it another way, so that it is more likely than not that an item of disrepair exists. Accordingly it is the surveyor's function to express his opinion on a balance of probabilities (or if appropriate on a high balance of probabilities) that a certain item is in disrepair. Certainty is not required in civil cases. Expressions such as "likely", or "very likely" are both acceptable as these are an alternative way of expressing a balance of probabilities.

The repairing covenant in the tenancy agreement

If the surveyor has been provided with a copy of the tenancy agreement either by the solicitor who instructs him, or by the tenant on the survey inspection, it is worth checking what the wording of the landlord's repairing covenant is. It will often be seen that the express repairing covenant goes further than the one which is implied by section 11 of the 1985 Act. The 1985 Act refers to "the dwelling house". Landlords often unwittingly impose higher repairing obligations on themselves by using more user-friendly language. Instead of referring to the dwelling house, they often refer to *"your home"*, or *"the premises"*, or *"the property"*. These are all much larger concepts in law than dwelling house, and would cover items such as, for example, garden fencing or walling, pathways and areas of hardstanding, or even outhouses. None of these could properly be described as being part of the dwelling house but would certainly be part of the premises, the property or the tenant's home. Accordingly if disrepair is found in any of these items, it would be actionable disrepair.

The Scott Schedule

The most important part of the surveyor's report is the Scott Schedule. Again it is a matter of style, but it is suggested that it is unnecessary to deal with the items of disrepair in the body of the report, as this is simply duplication both for the surveyor and for the lawyers, and perhaps ultimately for the judge. Nobody, especially the judge, wants to keep cross referring between the Scott Schedule and the body of the report. Within reason, it does not matter particularly how long the Scott Schedule is as long as all the material goes in the relevant columns. It is however a schedule and should serve the purpose of a schedule.

If however the surveyor feels that elaboration, further detail, or commentary is required in relation to a particular item of disrepair, then the appropriate place to do that is in the body of the report and not in the Scott Schedule. The Scott Schedule can refer the reader to the body of the report for the further detail or commentary.

Causation

Critical in these cases is the concept of causation. Put plainly, what is it that has caused the disrepair? Accordingly it will be necessary to state in the Scott Schedule what has caused the item in question to be in disrepair. Essentially this will be to rule out the possibility that the disrepair has been caused by the tenant's inappropriate use and occupation of the dwelling house e.g. purposely causing damage, or failing to report an item of disrepair which is damaging the property, such as a leaking pipe which is ruining plasterwork or woodwork.

This is embodied in section 11 (2) of the Landlord and Tenant Act 1985 which reads:

> *"The covenant implied by subsection (1) ("the lessor's repairing covenant") shall not be construed as requiring the lessor –*

(a) to carry out works for repairs for which the lessee is liable by virtue of his duty to use the premises in a tenant-like manner, or would be so liable but for an express covenant on his part,

(b) to rebuild or reinstate the premises in the case of destruction or damage by fire, or… other inevitable accident……"

If it is impossible to express an opinion on causation, even on the balance of probabilities, then the surveyor should make it clear what further investigations are needed before an opinion on causation can be expressed. It should however be remembered that firstly, further investigations come at a cost which the solicitor who is instructing may not want to incur unless it is absolutely necessary, and secondly, some investigations which are destructive – such as calcium carbide "speedy" tests can only be carried out with the permission of the landlord, because they are destructive. Given these limitations, if it is possible to express an opinion on causation on a balance of probabilities, then that is what should be done.

It might be that relatively simple tests like chloride and/or nitrate tests would help in determining the nature of dampness in a dwelling house, in which case these can be carried out with relative ease, and may prove definitive.

Further investigations should be very much the exception rather than the rule. Of course if an area of alleged disrepair is outwith the expertise of the surveyor – for example the opinion of the structural engineer is required – then that should be clearly stated in the report/Scott Schedule.

Once an opinion has been expressed by the Claimant's surveyor based on the balance of probabilities, the onus falls to the landlord to produce evidence of sufficient quality to gainsay that opinion.

Additional items

If in the course of a survey a surveyor comes across items of disrepair which are not included in the letter of claim (of which he will almost always have a copy as part of his instructions), then these should be included in the Scott Schedule under a separate heading such as "Additional items found on inspection". Paragraph 7.1 (d) of the Protocol states that the expert should be instructed to report on all items of disrepair which the landlord ought reasonably to know about, or which the expert ought reasonably to report on. This is important when read in conjunction with paragraph 6.5 of the Protocol which makes it clear that the letter of claim and the landlord's response are not intended to have the same status as a statement of case in court proceedings. Matters may come to light subsequently which means that the case of one or both parties may be presented differently in court proceedings. The Protocol also states that parties should not seek to take advantage of such discrepancies provided there was no intention to mislead. For convenience the Pre-Action Protocol for Housing Condition Cases (England) is set out in Appendix* of this book.

Condensation dampness

Condensation dampness as all surveyors will appreciate is an almost ubiquitous problem, certainly throughout the social housing sector. Sometimes condensation dampness and consequent black mould growth (aspilligus niger) arises as a result of the tenant's lifestyle i.e. the way in which the dwelling house is being used. Often this is from failing to ventilate the accommodation properly and/or failing to heat it properly. However sometimes (some may say often) the condensation and black mould growth problems are uncontrollable by the tenant. This is a critical distinction in housing conditions cases. Condensation problems which arise from tenant lifestyle will not be actionable, and will probably fall under the provisions of section 11 (2) of the 1985 Act discussed above (but subject of course to proof by the landlord), whereas others are actionable because the tenant has no control over the problem. For example, cold bridging because of a poor building design, insufficient insulation in the walls or in the roof space, the presence of rising or penetrating damp (or bridging) increasing the moisture in the atmosphere of the dwelling house, dilapidated or blown windows etc. All of these matters put a condensation problem beyond the control of the tenant and are therefore actionable. This should be made clear in the Scott Schedule.

The condensation problems may be actionable because they are an unavoidable corollary to disrepair and/or because they make a dwelling unfit for human habitation (see below). Accordingly it is essential for a surveyor to consider causation of condensation problems as they are so common and because they affect the life of the tenant and tenant's family on a daily basis. The problem is widespread throughout the social housing sector and seriously affects the lives of a large proportion of that sector. It not only damages property belonging to the tenant, but it is also well recognised as causing ill-health to the occupants. Again, an opinion expressed on the balance (or high balance) of probabilities will suffice in relation to causation.

It is extremely common for landlords as a default position to adopt the standpoint of blaming the tenant's lifestyle for condensation and mould problems. The housing Ombudsman has recently dealt with this in a special report issued on 26 October 2021 entitled "Spotlight on Damp and Mould". Importantly the Ombudsman said this:

> *"Our investigation heard immense frustration and sense of unfairness at the information sometimes provided to residents about issues like condensation. This occurred so often it is appropriate to call it systemic. The word "lifestyle", when it may be a consequence of limited choices, should be banished from the vernacular".*

This gives an important indication as to the seriousness of the problem, recently reinforced by the tragic and avoidable death in Rochdale of the 2-year old child Awaab Ishak due to physiological sequelae of long-term inhalation of black mould spores.

Condensation problems in a dwelling house therefore have to be considered carefully and thoroughly with clear opinions being expressed on causation. If the cause of the problems is both controllable by the tenant *and* uncontrollable, then the surveyor should state this in his report/Scott Schedule. However it is important in the context of litigation for an opinion to be expressed (even if it is a best "guestimate") as to the proportions of each in percentage terms. That part of the problem which is *uncontrollable* by the tenant would be actionable, and would sound in damages.

Unfitness for human habitation

On 20 March 2019 the new section 9A of the Landlord and Tenant Act 1985 came into force. It was inserted by the Homes (Fitness for Human Habitation) Act 2018. It applies to leases of dwellings in England granted on or after that date. For leases granted before 20 March 2019, the operative date for the provision is 20 March 2020.

Note that it applies to leases, as opposed to mere licences to occupy, and it applies to dwellings, not just to dwelling houses. It would encompass therefore any dwelling let on a lease, for example a static caravan or a houseboat.

As at the time of writing, there are no known recent authorities on unfitness for human habitation, and accordingly it is a question of fact for the judge in each case after hearing all of the evidence. Sometimes unfitness will be obvious, for example if there was no working toilet for more than a nominal period of time, no freshwater supply, no electricity supply, and no form of space heating. Conceivably, even these may fall into a grey area depending on the circumstances.

Other areas of unfitness will not be so clear. Surveyors must have a good working knowledge of sections 9A and 10 of the 1985 Act. Notably, it is a defence to the landlord under section 9A (3) if the unfitness for human habitation is wholly or mainly attributable to the tenant's own breach of covenant i.e. tenant's lifestyle and use and occupation of the dwelling.

The surveyor should therefore consider carefully causation for the housing conditions which allegedly make the dwelling unfit for human habitation.

Section 10 of the Act sets out the matters to which regard shall be had for the purposes of determining whether or not a dwelling is unfit for human habitation. The matters set out in the section are:

repair; stability; freedom from damp; internal arrangement; natural lighting; ventilation; water supply; drainage and sanitary conveniences; and facilities for preparation and cooking of food and for the disposal of waste water.

In addition, in relation to a dwelling in England, any prescribed hazard. Surveyors will be familiar with the (current) 29 prescribed hazards, and "prescribed hazard" is defined in section 10 (2) as meaning any matter or circumstance amounting to a hazard for the time being prescribed in Regulations made by the Secretary of State under section 2 of the Housing Act 2004.

It is to be noted that "hazard" means *any risk of harm to the health or safety of an actual occupier of a dwelling or house in multiple occupation which arises from a deficiency in the dwelling or house in multiple occupation or in any building or land in the vicinity (whether the deficiency arises as a result of the construction of any building, an absence of maintenance or repair, or otherwise).* As with section 11 (3A) of the 1985 Act, the duty under section 9A extends the duty to the building of which the dwelling forms part e.g. a flat in a block, or a room in a house of multiple occupation. It would also extend to the common parts where the landlord has retained an estate or interest in the part with the defect.

There is an important caveat which must be clearly understood by surveyors. The matters relevant to determining the question of unfitness must cross a certain threshold before they become relevant. Section 10 (1) of the Act says: "*… the house or dwelling shall be regarded as unfit for human habitation if, and only if, it is so far defective in one or more of those* *matters that it is not reasonably suitable for occupation in that condition"*. It is a question of fact for the trial judge whether that threshold is crossed in any particular dwelling, albeit that the opinion of the surveyor will be a relevant and may be an important factor. However it may be only one of a number of relevant factors.

Just as "disrepair" has been judicially defined (see above), various guidance has been given by judges over the years as to what may amount to unfitness. Rule of thumb guidance was given by Atkin LJ in *Morgan v Liverpool Corporation [1927] 2 KB 131 CA* and later approved in *Summers v Salford Corporation [1943] AC 283*. The guidance given was that if the state of repair of a house is such that by ordinary use damage may naturally be caused to the occupier, either in respect of personal injury to life or limb or injury to health, then the house is not in all respects reasonably fit for human habitation.

Further guidance was given in the more recent cases of *Rendlesham Estates plc and others v Barr Ltd [2015] 1 WLR 3663* and in *Bole and another v Huntsbuild Ltd [2009] EWCA Civ 1146 at page 34*. In *Rendlesham* examples were given of what may amount to unfitness, such as defective foundations; a lift which broke down with "monotonous regularity" taking into account the degree of inconvenience; no safe means of access or escape from a dwelling; hazards in the common parts; doors which did not meet building regulations for fire safety requirements; and mould and damp in living rooms and bedrooms.

It is suggested that the age and/or the general state of health of one or more of the occupants would be a relevant factor in determining whether, taken as a whole, a dwelling is unfit for human habitation.

Further considerations

If it appears to the surveyor that an item which falls within the landlord's express or implied repairing obligations has been in disrepair at least since the start of the tenancy, then this should be stated in the report/Scott Schedule. The reason for this is because there is not only an implied obligation to keep the dwelling house in repair, but there is also an obligation to put it into repair before the commencement of the tenancy. Accordingly, if on the balance of probabilities an item was in disrepair on the date on which the tenancy commenced, the landlord is imputed with notice irrespective of any notice given to it by the tenant at a later date.

It should always be remembered that just because an item which is in disrepair is not causing any discomfort or inconvenience to the tenant, it does not mean that that item is not in disrepair, and therefore not actionable. For example, a roof may have a number of slipped or missing slates but at that time, there may be no water ingress into the living accommodation, albeit in time there would be. The roof would undoubtedly be in disrepair at that point, but the tenant would not be entitled to any damages as the disrepair has at that time caused no discomfort or inconvenience. In spite of there then being no entitlement to damages for that particular matter, the disrepair must still appear in the surveyor's report/Scott Schedule. Disrepair, and damages for discomfort and inconvenience, are different concepts, albeit that often they are inextricably linked. Disrepair will more often than not give rise to a claim for damages, but not always.

Cavity wall insulation (CWI)

Surveyors should not forget to give thought to the possibility that CWI, if it has been installed, is in disrepair. The cavity and its contents are part of the structure of the dwelling house, and arguably a constituent part of its exterior. There may be voids in the CWI causing cold bridging, or it may have become damp, acting as a bridge to internal dampness. It may require professional removal and then to be reinstalled, or it may require simply to be removed, as it should never have been installed in the first place because it did not meet the various necessary criteria for installation.

As regards the cost of remedying disrepair, the Claimant's surveyor should state the market value i.e. the cost to the tenant of employing a regular contractor to have the work done. The reason for this is because the remedy of specific performance is an equitable (and therefore) discretionary remedy and it would in certain circumstances be appropriate for the tenant to ask the court to award damages in lieu of specific performance. This might occur, for example, where the landlord has repeatedly failed or neglected to carry out works of repair either which have been ordered by the court, or agreed in a compromise agreement (or Tomlin Order) between the parties. If that were to happen, the tenant would need to know, as would the court if appropriate, how much the tenant would need to be awarded in damages to have the work carried out by a private contractor. This sum is likely to be substantially more than would be the cost to the landlord who has the benefit of economy of scale, or its own workforce, or special arrangements with contractors on a commercial basis.

PART FOUR

MISCELLANEOUS

CHAPTER TWENTY-TWO

THE HOUSING OMBUDSMAN SERVICE

The Housing Ombudsman Service essentially provides a route for tenants to make a complaint about their landlord to an official body appointed by Parliament. Ombudsmen, as well as dealing with individual issues, also aim on occasions to identify systemic issues leading to poor service or breaches of peoples' rights.

An aggrieved tenant simply makes complaint by following the relevant procedure. The Ombudsman considers the factual matrix as described by the tenant and will seek such further information from the parties as is necessary to make a determination.

Essentially the Ombudsman's principal function is to decide whether there has been maladministration by the landlord and/or a service failure. He has various powers available if he finds maladministration (sometimes serious maladministration) and/or a service failure, and he can order the landlord to pay compensation or further compensation if it has already made an award to the tenant. If appropriate his decision may be that there is neither maladministration nor a service failure. In those circumstances the complaint would not be upheld.

The Ombudsman's decisions are published on the Ombudsman's website, www.housing-ombudsman.org.uk.

The decisions cover most if not all social landlords, with statistics as to how many findings there have been of maladministration or partial maladministration as well as findings of no maladministration, reasonable redress, mediation, or when the Housing Ombudsman

Service has no jurisdiction to hear the complaint. The statistics published usually run from 1st of April one year to 31st of March the next year.

The Ombudsman also publishes regular press releases dealing with findings of severe maladministration in relation to any particular housing association or local authority, and he also issues reports from time to time dealing with systemic issues – e.g. the report of 26 October 2021 – *"Spotlight on damp and mould – it's not lifestyle"*.

The number of findings against a particular landlord of maladministration and/or severe maladministration, and/or service failures, may influence some tenants who might be considering using the landlord's internal complaints procedure, to think twice before proceeding with a complaint.

The practical problems of complaining to the Housing Ombudsman Service

The Service is extremely overburdened with work and the problem is getting worse as complaints to the Service are growing at a very fast rate. The number of complaints received in 2022 was 137% higher than the previous year. This means that tenants can be waiting a long time, often more than a year, for a determination of their complaint. This is cold comfort to a tenant living in poor housing conditions which are causing very considerable discomfort and inconvenience, and possibly ill health to one or more of the occupants.

The level of awards of compensation made by the Ombudsman are rarely if ever comparable to those made by the courts. In real terms therefore an aggrieved tenant may be under-compensated for their justified grievance if they decide to go down this route. Similarly, unlike a decision in a court, the decision of the Ombudsman is not open to appeal. In some cases, this might lead to further cause for grievance.

The final problem for tenants is that the Ombudsman, unlike a court, cannot compel a landlord to carry out repairs. A court can make an order for specific performance pursuant to section 17 of the 1985 Act, but the Ombudsman has no such power. Accordingly, if the landlord fails to carry out repair work following a recommendation by the Ombudsman, the tenant has no redress other than to go back and make a further complaint to the Ombudsman. Again, cold comfort to tenants living in poor housing conditions, having already waited a long time even to have their complaint considered.

CONCLUSION

There is no doubt that there are many good and conscientious social landlords in the public housing sector. They genuinely care for the welfare of their tenants and do all that they reasonably can to ensure that their tenants have wholesome accommodation which provides good value for money and which is supported by a regime of effective complaint recording and a system for responsible and proactive repairs.

Unfortunately the converse is also true. There are many poorly and very poorly performing social landlords in the sector. There is a pervading culture of sloppiness at many levels, and an uncaring attitude towards their tenants whose lives are often made miserable as a result. They are living in inadequate housing conditions, and sometimes grossly inadequate housing conditions, causing frustration, anxiety and often illness in one form or another. One only has to look at the statistics reported by the Housing Ombudsman Service to see how many findings there are of service failures, maladministration, severe maladministration, and special reports on a number of poorly performing social landlords.

These poorly performing landlords may give a number of reasons for poor performance, but ultimately, it is suggested that this comes down to the unacceptable culture pervading the organisation, which filters down from the highest to the lowest levels.

There is a strong wind of change blowing – spearheaded both by the Housing Ombudsman as Regulator for Social Housing and the Government in the Social Housing (Regulation) Bill, which at the time of writing is still going through Parliament. It is to be earnestly hoped that between the new legislation and the Ombudsman, a new culture will emerge and meaningful and sustainable change will at last be brought to the public housing sector, thereby improving in every way the quality of the lives of many tenants and their families.

When litigation is required to reinforce that change, and a tenant needs to pursue a private law remedy, it is to be hoped that this practical guide will assist all professionals who are involved in the pursuit of that remedy.

MORE BOOKS BY LAW BRIEF PUBLISHING

A selection of our other titles available now:-

'A Practical Guide to Parental Alienation in Private and Public Law Children Cases' by Sam King QC & Frankie Shama
'Contested Heritage – Removing Art from Land and Historic Buildings' by Richard Harwood QC, Catherine Dobson, David Sawtell
'The Limits of Separate Legal Personality: When Those Running a Company Can Be Held Personally Liable for Losses Caused to Third Parties Outside of the Company' by Dr Mike Wilkinson
'A Practical Guide to Transgender Law' by Robin Moira White & Nicola Newbegin
'Artificial Intelligence – The Practical Legal Issues (2nd Edition)' by John Buyers
'A Practical Guide to Residential Freehold Conveyancing' by Lorraine Richardson
'A Practical Guide to Pensions on Divorce for Lawyers' by Bryan Scant
'A Practical Guide to Challenging Sham Marriage Allegations in Immigration Law' by Priya Solanki
'A Practical Guide to Legal Rights in Scotland' by Sarah-Jane Macdonald
'A Practical Guide to New Build Conveyancing' by Paul Sams & Rebecca East
'A Practical Guide to Defending Barristers in Disciplinary Cases' by Marc Beaumont
'A Practical Guide to Inherited Wealth on Divorce' by Hayley Trim
'A Practical Guide to Practice Direction 12J and Domestic Abuse in Private Law Children Proceedings' by Rebecca Cross & Malvika Jaganmohan
'A Practical Guide to Confiscation and Restraint' by Narita Bahra QC, John Carl Townsend, David Winch
'A Practical Guide to the Law of Forests in Scotland' by Philip Buchan
'A Practical Guide to Health and Medical Cases in Immigration Law' by Rebecca Chapman & Miranda Butler
'A Practical Guide to Bad Character Evidence for Criminal Practitioners by Aparna Rao
'A Practical Guide to Extradition Law post-Brexit' by Myles Grandison et al

'A Practical Guide to Hoarding and Mental Health for Housing Lawyers' by Rachel Coyle
'A Practical Guide to Psychiatric Claims in Personal Injury – 2nd Edition' by Liam Ryan
'Stephens on Contractual Indemnities' by Richard Stephens
'A Practical Guide to the EU Succession Regulation' by Richard Frimston
'A Practical Guide to Solicitor and Client Costs – 2nd Edition' by Robin Dunne
'Constructive Dismissal – Practice Pointers and Principles' by Benjimin Burgher
'A Practical Guide to Religion and Belief Discrimination Claims in the Workplace' by Kashif Ali
'A Practical Guide to the Law of Medical Treatment Decisions' by Ben Troke
'Fundamental Dishonesty and QOCS in Personal Injury Proceedings: Law and Practice' by Jake Rowley
'A Practical Guide to the Law in Relation to School Exclusions' by Charlotte Hadfield & Alice de Coverley
'A Practical Guide to Divorce for the Silver Separators' by Karin Walker
'The Right to be Forgotten – The Law and Practical Issues' by Melissa Stock
'A Practical Guide to Planning Law and Rights of Way in National Parks, the Broads and AONBs' by James Maurici QC, James Neill et al
'A Practical Guide to Election Law' by Tom Tabori
'A Practical Guide to the Law in Relation to Surrogacy' by Andrew Powell
'A Practical Guide to Claims Arising from Fatal Accidents – 2nd Edition' by James Patience
'A Practical Guide to the Ownership of Employee Inventions – From Entitlement to Compensation' by James Tumbridge & Ashley Roughton
'A Practical Guide to Asbestos Claims' by Jonathan Owen & Gareth McAloon
'A Practical Guide to Stamp Duty Land Tax in England and Northern Ireland' by Suzanne O'Hara
'A Practical Guide to the Law of Farming Partnerships' by Philip Whitcomb
'Covid-19, Homeworking and the Law – The Essential Guide to Employment and GDPR Issues' by Forbes Solicitors
'Covid-19 and Criminal Law – The Essential Guide' by Ramya Nagesh
'Covid-19 and Family Law in England and Wales – The Essential Guide' by Safda Mahmood

'A Practical Guide to the Law of Unlawful Eviction and Harassment – 2nd Edition' by Stephanie Lovegrove
'Covid-19, Brexit and the Law of Commercial Leases – The Essential Guide' by Mark Shelton
'A Practical Guide to Costs in Personal Injury Claims – 2nd Edition' by Matthew Hoe
'A Practical Guide to the General Data Protection Regulation (GDPR) – 2nd Edition' by Keith Markham
'Ellis on Credit Hire – Sixth Edition' by Aidan Ellis & Tim Kevan
'A Practical Guide to Working with Litigants in Person and McKenzie Friends in Family Cases' by Stuart Barlow
'Protecting Unregistered Brands: A Practical Guide to the Law of Passing Off' by Lorna Brazell
'A Practical Guide to Secondary Liability and Joint Enterprise Post-Jogee' by Joanne Cecil & James Mehigan
'A Practical Guide to the Pre-Action RTA Claims Protocol for Personal Injury Lawyers' by Antonia Ford
'A Practical Guide to Neighbour Disputes and the Law' by Alexander Walsh
'A Practical Guide to Forfeiture of Leases' by Mark Shelton
'A Practical Guide to Coercive Control for Legal Practitioners and Victims' by Rachel Horman
'A Practical Guide to Rights Over Airspace and Subsoil' by Daniel Gatty
'Tackling Disclosure in the Criminal Courts – A Practitioner's Guide' by Narita Bahra QC & Don Ramble
'A Practical Guide to the Law of Driverless Cars – Second Edition' by Alex Glassbrook, Emma Northey & Scarlett Milligan
'A Practical Guide to TOLATA Claims' by Greg Williams
'A Practical Guide to Elderly Law – 2nd Edition' by Justin Patten
'A Practical Guide to Responding to Housing Disrepair and Unfitness Claims' by Iain Wightwick
'A Practical Guide to the Construction and Rectification of Wills and Trust Instruments' by Edward Hewitt
'A Practical Guide to the Law of Bullying and Harassment in the Workplace' by Philip Hyland
'How to Be a Freelance Solicitor: A Practical Guide to the SRA-Regulated Freelance Solicitor Model' by Paul Bennett

'A Practical Guide to Prison Injury Claims' by Malcolm Johnson
'A Practical Guide to the Small Claims Track - 2nd Edition' by Dominic Bright
'A Practical Guide to Advising Clients at the Police Station' by Colin Stephen McKeown-Beaumont
'A Practical Guide to Antisocial Behaviour Injunctions' by Iain Wightwick
'Practical Mediation: A Guide for Mediators, Advocates, Advisers, Lawyers, and Students in Civil, Commercial, Business, Property, Workplace, and Employment Cases' by Jonathan Dingle with John Sephton
'The Mini-Pupillage Workbook' by David Boyle
'A Practical Guide to Crofting Law' by Brian Inkster
'A Practical Guide to Spousal Maintenance' by Liz Cowell
'A Practical Guide to the Law of Domain Names and Cybersquatting' by Andrew Clemson
'A Practical Guide to the Law of Gender Pay Gap Reporting' by Harini Iyengar
'A Practical Guide to the Rights of Grandparents in Children Proceedings' by Stuart Barlow
'NHS Whistleblowing and the Law' by Joseph England
'Employment Law and the Gig Economy' by Nigel Mackay & Annie Powell
'A Practical Guide to Noise Induced Hearing Loss (NIHL) Claims' by Andrew Mckie, Ian Skeate, Gareth McAloon
'An Introduction to Beauty Negligence Claims – A Practical Guide for the Personal Injury Practitioner' by Greg Almond
'Intercompany Agreements for Transfer Pricing Compliance' by Paul Sutton
'Zen and the Art of Mediation' by Martin Plowman
'A Practical Guide to the SRA Principles, Individual and Law Firm Codes of Conduct 2019 – What Every Law Firm Needs to Know' by Paul Bennett
'A Practical Guide to Adoption for Family Lawyers' by Graham Pegg
'A Practical Guide to Industrial Disease Claims' by Andrew Mckie & Ian Skeate
'A Practical Guide to Redundancy' by Philip Hyland
'A Practical Guide to Vicarious Liability' by Mariel Irvine
'A Practical Guide to Applications for Landlord's Consent and Variation of Leases' by Mark Shelton
'A Practical Guide to Relief from Sanctions Post-Mitchell and Denton' by Peter Causton

'A Practical Guide to Equity Release for Advisors' by Paul Sams
'A Practical Guide to Financial Services Claims' by Chris Hegarty
'The Law of Houses in Multiple Occupation: A Practical Guide to HMO Proceedings' by Julian Hunt
'Occupiers, Highways and Defective Premises Claims: A Practical Guide Post-Jackson – 2nd Edition' by Andrew Mckie
'A Practical Guide to Financial Ombudsman Service Claims' by Adam Temple & Robert Scrivenor
'A Practical Guide to Advising Schools on Employment Law' by Jonathan Holden
'A Practical Guide to Running Housing Disrepair and Cavity Wall Claims: 2nd Edition' by Andrew Mckie & Ian Skeate
'A Practical Guide to Holiday Sickness Claims – 2nd Edition' by Andrew Mckie & Ian Skeate
'Arguments and Tactics for Personal Injury and Clinical Negligence Claims' by Dorian Williams
'A Practical Guide to Drone Law' by Rufus Ballaster, Andrew Firman, Eleanor Clot
'A Practical Guide to Compliance for Personal Injury Firms Working With Claims Management Companies' by Paul Bennett
'RTA Allegations of Fraud in a Post-Jackson Era: The Handbook – 2nd Edition' by Andrew Mckie
'RTA Personal Injury Claims: A Practical Guide Post-Jackson' by Andrew Mckie
'On Experts: CPR35 for Lawyers and Experts' by David Boyle
'An Introduction to Personal Injury Law' by David Boyle

These books and more are available to order online direct from the publisher at www.lawbriefpublishing.com, where you can also read free sample chapters. For any queries, contact us on 0844 587 2383 or mail@lawbriefpublishing.com.

Our books are also usually in stock at www.amazon.co.uk with free next day delivery for Prime members, and at good legal bookshops such as Wildy & Sons.

We are regularly launching new books in our series of practical day-to-day practitioners' guides. Visit our website and join our free newsletter to be kept informed and to receive special offers, free chapters, etc.

You can also follow us on Twitter at www.twitter.com/lawbriefpub.

www.ingramcontent.com/pod-product-compliance
Lightning Source LLC
LaVergne TN
LVHW022109200926
848481LV00003B/1115
* 9 7 8 1 9 1 4 6 0 8 9 2 6 *